THE

RULES

OF

EVERYTHING

Pearson

At Pearson, we have a simple mission: to help people make more of their lives through learning.

We combine innovative learning technology with trusted content and educational expertise to provide engaging and effective learning experiences that serve people wherever and whenever they are learning.

From classroom to boardroom, our curriculum materials, digital learning tools and testing programmes help to educate millions of people worldwide – more than any other private enterprise.

Every day our work helps learning flourish, and wherever learning flourishes, so do people.

To learn more, please visit us at **www.pearson.com/uk**

THE
RULES
OF
EVERYTHING

A complete code for success
and happiness in everything
that matters

RICHARD TEMPLAR

Pearson

Harlow, England • London • New York • Boston • San Francisco • Toronto • Sydney
Dubai • Singapore • Hong Kong • Tokyo • Seoul • Taipei • New Delhi
Cape Town • São Paulo • Mexico City • Madrid • Amsterdam • Munich • Paris • Milan

PEARSON EDUCATION LIMITED
KAO Two
KAO Park
Harlow CM17 9NA
United Kingdom
Tel: +44 (0)1279 623623
Web: www.pearson.com/uk

First edition published 2022 (print and electronic)

ISBN: 978-1-292-43212-0 (print)
      978-1-292-43214-4 (PDF)
      978-1-292-43213-7 (ePub)

British Library Cataloguing-in-Publication Data
A catalogue record for the print edition is available from the British Library

Library of Congress Cataloging-in-Publication Data
A catalog record for the print edition is available from the Library of Congress

10 9 8 7 6 5 4 3 2 1
26 25 24 23 22

Cover design by Nick Redeyoff

Print edition typeset in 11/13pt ITC Berkeley Oldstyle Pro by Straive
Printed in the UK by Bell and Bain Ltd, Glasgow

NOTE THAT ANY PAGE CROSS REFERENCES REFER TO THE PRINT EDITION

Contents

The Rules of Life 50

The Rules of Wealth 74

The Rules of Parenting 98

The Rules of Love 122

The Rules of Living Well 218

Know When to Break the Rules 242

Pearson's Commitment to Diversity, Equity and Inclusion

Pearson is dedicated to creating bias-free content that reflects the diversity, depth and breadth of all learners' lived experiences. We embrace the many dimensions of diversity including, but not limited to, race, ethnicity, gender, sex, sexual orientation, socioeconomic status, ability, age and religious or political beliefs.

Education is a powerful force for equity and change in our world. It has the potential to deliver opportunities that improve lives and enable economic mobility. As we work with authors to create content for every product and service, we acknowledge our responsibility to demonstrate inclusivity and incorporate diverse scholarship so that everyone can achieve their potential through learning. As the world's leading learning company, we have a duty to help drive change and live up to our purpose to help more people create a better life for themselves and to create a better world.

Our ambition is to purposefully contribute to a world where:

- Everyone has an equitable and lifelong opportunity to succeed through learning.
- Our educational products and services are inclusive and represent the rich diversity of learners.
- Our educational content accurately reflects the histories and lived experiences of the learners we serve.
- Our educational content prompts deeper discussions with students and motivates them to expand their own learning and worldview.

We are also committed to providing products that are fully accessible to all learners. As per Pearson's guidelines for accessible educational Web media, we test and retest the capabilities of our products against the highest standards for every release, following the WCAG guidelines in developing new products for copyright year 2022 and beyond. You can learn more about Pearson's commitment to accessibility at:

https://www.pearson.com/us/accessibility.html

While we work hard to present unbiased, fully accessible content, we want to hear from you about any concerns or needs regarding this Pearson product so that we can investigate and address them.

- Please contact us with concerns about any potential bias at:

  https://www.pearson.com/report-bias.html

- For accessibility-related issues, such as using assistive technology with Pearson products, alternative text requests, or accessibility documentation, email the Pearson Disability Support team at:

  disability.support@pearson

Acknowledgements

Over the years, countless people have given me ideas, and feedback about their favourite Rules, via messages, emails and reviews. I'm extremely grateful to them all for their reflections on which Rules have especially resonated with them or worked for them. Among them have been the many readers who follow my Facebook page, and I'd like to say a very particular thank you to:

Abiboulaye Diouf

Aimee Mullin

Alicia Hattingh and Donna the pizza lady

Andrew Green

Andy Cheung

Andy Sims

Anil Baddela

Anna Odell

Ashley Creighton

Baran R Ahmed

Bolaji Fesomade

Carol Ingram

Charmaine Gilmour

Chuka Kizito Igbokwe

Chukwudimma Okolo

Damilola Akinwande

Daniel Nortey

Davey Blair

David Grigor

De Krawn

Debra Pennington-Bick

Ela Augustyniak

Elie Williams

Elif Vatanoğlu

Ernest Tay

Esme Holburt

Frank Hull

Glendon Hall

Hal Craze

Harold T White

Haya Bashir

Hubert Rau

Ibrahim Aar

Ibtihal Souici

Ismail Ahmed

Jalaj Soni

Jimmy Ling

Jo BW

John James Fitzgerald

Johnson Grace Maganja
Joyce SP Siaw
King Nkandu
KJ Carleo
Leepin Tan
Lynn Mercer
Maria Andrade
Maira Shaikh
Mariska Slagmoolen
Martin Langham
Mdooter Saasongo
Mi Chel Le
Michael Bingley
Mogana Raman
Mohamed Aboud Cfm Cerifr
Ndubuisi Chibueze
Neil Duggan
Nick Saunders
Nicola Betts
Nicole Shum
Nikki Betts
Octavia Craze

Olabisi Adebule
Pawan Singh
Pommie Flower
Rachael Stock
Rol Vicente Guevara
Rolin Roy Guevara Jnr
Salisu Muazu
Sarah McCoy
Sarah-Jane Monro
Shahrin Zubair
Sharon McCoy
Skaff Nel
Szöllősi Bernadett
Tina Steel
Victoria Wen
Virginia Josey
Virginia Wan
Walid Ali
Yan Or
Yana del Ray
Zakia Moulaoui

Introduction

Welcome to *The Rules of Everything*. It's a pretty grand sounding title, eh? So... *everything*? OK, these aren't all the Rules there ever are or could be, but they do cover pretty much every area of life – your life, my life, everyone's life.

Rules? What *are* Rules with a capital R? Well, nearly 20 years ago I wrote a book called *The Rules of Work*, which covered 100 or so of the most important unwritten Rules that are essential for your career, but no one tells you. Attitudes and mindsets you need to follow. I'm one of life's people watchers and these were all principles I'd observed during my working life, and which I'd copied successfully myself. Eventually I left the full-time corporate world to pursue other things, including writing. That was when it had dawned on me that other people might be interested in these hidden Rules, so I began to write them down ... and *The Rules of Work* was born. A few of them are unexpected or surprising, but most of them are common sense when you think about it. However most of us don't think about it in the hurly-burly of everything else, which is why bringing them all together in one book seemed a good idea. They're more of a reminder than a revelation.

The Rules of Work was way more successful than I ever imagined – it turned out that an awful lot of people could see the value they could get from it, and I was delighted when I started to hear from readers whose careers had taken off once they too started to practise the Rules. So I wrote *The Rules of Management*. From there the series built up, through *Life, Wealth, Parenting, Love...* and there are now ten books in the series which, between them, really do cover pretty much everything.

So now seemed like the obvious time to put together the best of the best. Regular Rules readers know that it's well worth investing in a book that gives you 100+ Rules about a key part of your life. But not everyone is a parent, or works in management, or is aiming to be really wealthy, and ten books is a big investment when the topics aren't central to your life at the moment. However, that doesn't mean you don't want to learn any of those Rules. So here we have the top ten Rules from each book brought together in one volume so you have an overview of the Rules of everything.

I'm sensing you want to know who decides which are the top ten Rules from each book? I wanted to know that too, when I decided to bring together this compilation. So I asked the obvious people – the readers. All those Rules Players who have been buying the books over the years, not just in the UK where they were first published, but around the world. I hear from people in Iraq, Thailand, Brazil, the US, Uganda, India, Europe … so I looked at their messages and posts, and I asked all the readers who follow my Facebook page to tell me what their very favourite Rules were.

Once the votes were in and counted, I had my top ten Rules for each book. Oh alright, it wasn't quite that straightforward and I had to curate it a bit. There wasn't always an obvious cut-off at ten, for example. There might be six or seven standout Rules for a particular book, followed by half a dozen that all got the same number of votes, so I had to make a decision on which of those to include. Also, I wanted to bring you a good cross-section of each book, so where all the top votes fell in the same section of the book, I selected a couple from elsewhere. For example, most people's favourite Rules in *The Rules of Love* are from the categories about finding love, or about romantic partnerships. However there are also sections on family and friends and so on, so I've respected the overall balance towards romance but I've given you the odd popular Rule from those other sections too. *The Rules of Everything* needs to give you a useful selection of Rules in itself – that's the whole point – so I had to take this into account. This selection is very much focused on readers' favourite Rules, but with a bit of curating to make it as useful a volume as possible.

For the benefit of any regular readers who know about these things, I would add that I haven't included Rules from the extra sections that have been added to the books. More recent editions have an extra ten Rules on a related subject – for example there are ten Rules of happiness at the end of *The Rules of Life*, and ten Rules to follow at the end of *The Rules to Break*. It was too confusing to include these because only people who have bought later editions have seen them, and of course they're only tangential to the subject of the book.

There are ten sections here, one for each of the individual books. I did think about what order to put them in but, in the end, the order of publication seemed as good as any. So I started with *The Rules of Work* and went from there. Within those sections I defaulted at ordering the Rules in the order they appear in the book itself, but I've tinkered with this where a better order presented itself, for example putting related Rules next to each other.

I can't tell you how much I've enjoyed putting this together and finding out which are the Rules that have most struck a chord with readers over the years. If you want to share your favourite Rules with me – either from my books or Rules you've observed yourself (I don't have a monopoly) – please get in touch via my Facebook page.

Richard Templar

www.facebook.com/richardtemplar

How to use the Rules

It can be a bit daunting to read a book with 100 Rules for a happier more successful life. I mean, where do you start? You'll probably find you follow a few of them already, but how can you be expected to learn dozens of new Rules all at once and start putting them all into practice? Don't panic, you don't have to. Remember, you don't *have* to do anything – you're doing this because you want to. Let's keep it at a manageable level so you go on wanting to.

You can go about this any way you like but, if you want advice, here's what I recommend. Go through the book and pick out three or four Rules that you feel would make a big difference to you, or that jumped out at you when you first read them, or that seem like a good starting point for you. Write them down here:

Just work on these for a couple of weeks until they've become ingrained and you don't have to try so hard with them. They've become a habit. Great stuff, well done. Now you can repeat the exercise with a few more Rules you'd like to tackle next. Write them here:

Excellent. Now you're really making progress. Keep working through the Rules at your own pace – there's no rush. Before long you'll find you're really getting on top of all the Rules that will help you, and more and more of them are becoming ingrained. And voilà, congratulations – you're a proper Rules Player.

THE RULES OF
WORK

The Rules of Work was the very first Rules book. I'd spent decades working in the kind of organisations that employed dozens, hundreds or even thousands of people, in some kind of hierarchical structure. Pretty much everyone in these organisations aspires to climb the corporate ladder, but logic tells you that with far fewer people at the top than at the bottom, most people won't make it. Over the years I'd worked out that the trick – beyond being very good at your job – was to understand the unspoken rules: the ones that no one tells you, but which the people at the top of these companies had followed in order to get where they were.

I'd taken to watching what these people did and didn't do, in common with each other, to make sure they succeeded, that they got noticed, that they were spoken of with respect and admiration. So I started to do these same things and, lo and behold, I started to find myself being moved up the hierarchy. Sometimes I even leapfrogged entire levels of management, or ended up supervising someone who used to be my boss. And all because I learnt to follow the Rules.

The Rules of Work is divided into ten sections:

- Walk your talk

- Know that you're being judged at all times

- Have a plan

- If you can't say anything nice – shut up

- Look after yourself

- Blend in

- Act one step ahead

- Cultivate diplomacy

- Know the system – and milk it

- Handle the opposition.

It's a funny thing, I thought I'd have to edit out several Rules – all the ones that involved being underhand or back-stabbing or downright crooked. But when I analysed the people I've known over the years who had used these methods, almost none of them had been successful. Of course you could point at the odd exception, but I'd seen people come a cropper using those methods far more frequently than the odd one I'd seen climb the ladder that way.

So the ten Rules that follow are those that Rules readers and I consider the most useful. Incidentally, the top-voted Rule in this section was 'Under promise and over deliver', a classic Rule. It's from the 'Walk your talk' section, which was particularly popular with readers. Rules from 'If you can't say anything nice – shut up' also got more than their share of votes, led by 'Don't gossip'.

Get your work noticed

It's all too easy for your work to get overlooked in the busy hurly-burly of office life. You're slaving away and it can be hard to remember that you need to put in some effort to boost your individual status and personal kudos for your work. But it's important. You have to make your mark so you stand out and your promotional potential will be realised.

The best way to do this is to step outside the normal working routine. If you have to process so many widgets each day – and so does everyone else – then processing more won't do you that much good. But if you submit a report to your boss of how *everyone* could process more widgets then you'll get noticed. The unsolicited report is a brilliant way to stand out from the crowd. It shows you're thinking on your feet and using your initiative. But it mustn't be used too often. If you subject your boss to a barrage of unsolicited reports, you'll get noticed but in completely the wrong way. You have to stick to certain rules:

- Only submit a report occasionally.
- Make really sure that your report will actually work – that it will do good or provide benefits.
- Make sure your name is prominently displayed.
- Make sure the report will be seen not only by your boss, but by their boss as well.
- Remember it doesn't have to be a report – it can be an article in the company newsletter.

Of course, the very best way to get your work noticed is to be very, very good at your job. And the best way to be good at your job is to be totally dedicated to doing the job and ignoring all the rest. There is a vast amount of politics, gossip, gamesmanship, time wasting and socialising that goes on in the name of work. It isn't work. Keep your eye on the ball and you'll already be playing with a vast advantage over your colleagues. The Rules Player stays focused. Keep your mind on the task at hand – being very good at your job – and don't get distracted.

> ## THE UNSOLICITED REPORT IS A BRILLIANT WAY TO STAND OUT FROM THE CROWD

Never let anyone know how hard you work

Look at someone like Richard Branson. He is always seen as playing, flying balloons, living on a converted barge, flying to the States. You never see him sitting at a desk, answering phones, doing paperwork. But at some time during his working day that is exactly what he must do. We just don't get to see it. Thus we think of him as the business playboy, the happy-go-lucky entrepreneur, the devilish entertainer. It's a neat image and one that he seems very happy to go along with – and why not?

This is the sort of image the intrepid Rules Player wants to cultivate – suave, easy, relaxed, languid, in control and very chilled. You never run, never panic, never even seem to hurry. Yes, you may stay up until the early hours of every morning but you will never admit this, never let on, never moan about how hard you work or the hours you put in. To the outside observer you are coasting, taking it easy, taking it all in your stride.

Obviously, to be able to do this you have to be very good at your job. If you ain't, then you're going to come a cropper trying this Rule out for size. So, what do you do if you aren't very good at your job? Burn that midnight oil again getting good. Learn, study, gain experience and knowledge, read, ask questions, revise, swot and cram until you do know that job inside and out. Do this first and then you can swan about looking cool and very relaxed.

There are a few rules within this Rule:

- Never ask for an extension of a deadline.

- Never ask for help: never admit that you are out of your depth – you can ask for guidance, advice, information, an opinion, but never help.

- Never moan or complain about how much work you have to do.

- Learn to be assertive so you don't get overloaded – this is not about letting others know how hard you do work, but you don't have to overdo it and overwork.

- Never be seen breaking into a sweat.

- Always look for ways to ease your workload – unnoticed of course – and ways to speed things up.

> **TO BE ABLE TO DO THIS**
>
> **YOU HAVE TO BE VERY**
>
> **GOOD AT YOUR JOB**

Set personal standards

Do you sleep at night? I know I do, but then I set personal standards that I simply won't break.

- I will not knowingly hurt or hinder another human being in the pursuit of my career.
- I will not knowingly break any laws in the furtherance of my career.
- I will have a moral code that I will follow no matter what.
- I will endeavour to provide a positive contribution to society by what I do for a living.
- I will not do anything that I would be ashamed to talk to my children about.
- I will put my family first at all times.
- I will not work evenings or weekends, unless it is an emergency and I have discussed it with my partner.
- I will not unfairly stitch up anyone in my pursuit of new work.
- I will always endeavour to put something back.
- I will pass on freely and openly any skills, knowledge or experience to anyone who could use them to benefit themselves within the same industry – I won't hog information for the sake of it.
- I will not be jealous of anyone else's success in the same industry.
- I will question the long-term ramifications of what I do constantly.
- I will play by the Rules at all times.

This code of conduct is my own personal set of standards. It might not suit you. You may need or have a better set. I do hope you don't opt for a worse one. We must endeavour to be the very, very best we can at all times.

> # WE MUST ENDEAVOUR TO BE THE VERY, VERY BEST WE CAN AT ALL TIMES

RULE 4

Carve out a niche for yourself

I once worked with a colleague who made it a great personal skill to find out stuff about customers that we couldn't. It seemed he always knew the names of their children, where they took their holidays, their birthdays – and their spouses' – their favourite music and restaurants, and consequently if you had to deal with a particular customer you went to Mike and asked, politely and humbly, if he could give you some little titbit that would get you well in with the customer. Mike had carved out a niche for himself. No one asked him to become a walking encyclopaedia of customer likes and dislikes. It wasn't part of his job description. It took a lot of work and unseen effort. And it was a very valuable asset. It didn't take long for the regional director to hear of this extra effort Mike had put in and his rise up the corporate ladder was swift, meteoric, unprecedented. That's all it took. I say 'all', it was in fact a lot of work and immensely clever.

Carving out a niche means spotting a useful area that no one else has spotted. It might be as simple as being great at spreadsheets or report writing. It might be, like Mike, knowing something no one else does. It might be being brilliant with rotas or budgets or understanding the system. Make sure you don't make yourself indispensable or this Rule backfires.

Carving out a niche for yourself often takes you out of the normal range of office activities. You get to move around more, be out of the office more often without having to explain to anyone where you are or what you are doing. This makes you stand out from the herd, gives you independence and a superior quality. I once volunteered to edit the company newsletter – bearing in mind the previous Rule – and could wander about between our seven branches at will. Obviously, I always made sure my work was done on time and supremely well.

Carving out a niche for yourself frequently means you get noticed by people other than your boss – other people's bosses. These bosses get together and they talk. If they bring your name up it will be in a good way – 'I see Rich has been busy doing some really original market analysis'. This makes it difficult for your boss not to promote you if they want to win their peer group approval. If the other bosses think you are a good idea then your boss really has to go along with it.

> # IF THE OTHER BOSSES THINK YOU ARE A GOOD IDEA THEN YOUR BOSS REALLY HAS TO GO ALONG WITH IT

RULE 5

Under promise and over deliver

If you know you can do it by Wednesday always say Friday. If you know it will take your department a week, say two. If you know it will cost an extra two people to get the new machine installed and up and running, then say three.

This isn't dishonest, merely prudent. If it gets spotted that this is what you do, then openly and honestly admit it and say you always build a contingency percentage into your calculations. They can't kill you for that.

That's the first bit. Under promise. And just because you have said Friday or two weeks or whatever doesn't mean you can coast and use up that allowance. Oh no. What you have to do is make sure you deliver early, on budget and better than promised. And that's the second part. Over deliver. This means if you promised to have the report finished by Monday first thing, it is finished, but not only is it a report, it also contains the full implementation plans for the new premises. Or if you said you'd have the exhibition stand up and running by Sunday night with only two extra members of staff, you have – and you've managed to get your major competitor to pull out of the show. Or if you said you'd have a rough proposal written for the new company website by the next meeting you not only have this but also a site map, sample graphics, the text drafted, all the photos taken and full design costs and SEO proposal. Obviously, you've got to be careful that you don't overstep the mark and assume responsibilities you haven't been given, but I'm sure you get the idea.

Again, it might be stating the obvious but don't be too blatant when you do this or your boss will get to expect it – it should be a pleasant surprise not a frequently used tactic.

It also helps sometimes to act dumb. You can pretend you don't really understand some new technique or software when in reality you know it back to front. Then when you suddenly do all the budgets on the spreadsheets that no one else could, you look good. If, in advance, you had said 'Oh, yes, I know that, I worked with these spreadsheets at my last place', there is no surprise and you've given the game away – and your advantage.

When you under promise and over deliver you have to have a bottom line – in your case, as a Rules Player, it is simply that you will *never* deliver late or deliver short. That's it. If you have to sweat blood and work all night then so be it. You will deliver when you said you would – or earlier if you can – without exception. It is better to negotiate a longer delivery time in the first place than to have to let someone down. A lot of people are so keen to be liked, or approved of, or praised that they will agree to the first delivery time offered to them – 'Oh yes, I can do that', and then they fail. They look like pushovers in the first place and incompetent in the last.

> # YOU WILL *NEVER* DELIVER
> # LATE OR DELIVER SHORT

RULE 6

Know what you want long term

So what's your game plan for your life? Don't know? Haven't ever thought about it? Most people don't. And that's why they fail. If you don't have a plan, it is terribly easy not to stick to it and end up where the current takes you – a bit of flotsam adrift on the eddies of life, very sad. The Rules Player has a plan – long term and short term.

Long-term plans can be very simple – qualify, move up, reach the top, retire, die. Or they can be sensible and useful. If you intend having a career, it makes sense to study the game plan of your chosen industry. Obviously, you will have to build in a certain contingency for the unexpected and the 'out-of-your-control', but the shrewd Rules Player will have already amended their long-term game plan well in advance having seen the indicators and read the signs. I spoke to someone recently who said, 'Who would have predicted downsizing then?' The answer is anyone with the brains to have seen which way their business sector was going.

So, study your chosen industry and see the progression steps needed to make it to the position you want to occupy. Work out what you need to make those steps. Work out how many steps it takes – usually no more than about four – junior, middle, senior, executive. (If you think otherwise don't write in.)

Work out what you want from each step – gaining experience, handling responsibility, learning new skills, acquiring people management understanding, that sort of thing. You will notice that 'increasing my earnings' just isn't an option here – that is a foregone conclusion if you are a Rules Player anyway.

Work out how each step is made. This might be a transfer to another department, relocation to another branch, being offered a partnership, being invited to join the board, moving to another company, that sort of thing. Once you know how each step is made, it doesn't take much to work out what you need to acquire that *how*.

You have to have an end game – the final goal. This can be as high or as extreme as you like – empress of the world, prime minister, CEO, wealthiest person in the world, whatever. It is a dream and thus has no limits. If you set limits on your imagination, then you will have to settle for less than the best, less than perfect, less than you deserve. Ah, but you say we have to be realistic. Fine, do that, be realistic. But a Rules Player heads for the very utmost of their dreams and nothing less than the top is good enough.

> IF YOU DON'T HAVE A PLAN,
> IT IS TERRIBLY EASY NOT TO
> STICK TO IT AND END UP
> WHERE THE CURRENT
> TAKES YOU

Don't gossip

'Did you know that at the last company conference Raj, from accounts, was seen coming out of Debbie's, from marketing, bedroom in the early hours of Sunday morning? And that's twice they have been seen in Luigi's at lunchtime and Kathy swears she's seen them holding hands in the lift. Raj is married, you know, and I thought Debbie was engaged. What do you think? Should they be carrying on like this?'

Answer: 'What's this got to do with me?'

Good, it has nothing to do with you, unless Raj happens to be your boss and his work is being affected, or you happen to be Debbie's fiancé. This Rule says that you don't gossip. It doesn't say you don't listen. You may find it interesting and knowing what's going on comes in useful sometimes. But there is one part of this Rule that is really, really simple – don't pass anything on. That's it. Gossip stops with you. If you listen but don't pass it along or offer an opinion, you'll be seen as 'one of us' rather than a party pooper. You don't have to be seen to be disapproving – merely don't pass anything along.

Gossiping is the occupation of idle minds – those who haven't got enough work to do. It is also the domain of workers who have mindless jobs to do – jobs they can do without thinking and thus have to occupy themselves with inane chatter, tittle tattle, rumour, lies and malicious stories. Trouble is that if you don't join in, you can be seen as severe or stuck up. You have to look as if you gossip without ever doing it. Don't go getting all hoity-toity and telling everyone how silly they are doing it.

With most things discretion is the key word. Don't be seen disapproving – just don't do it and keep that to yourself. Over time, people will notice that secrets stop with you, and that in itself will work in your favour. Not only will they respect you, they may also confide in you. You will never abuse these confidences, but if you can make use of them without undermining the person who told you, well, that can sometimes work in your favour too.

> **THERE IS ONE PART OF THIS RULE THAT IS REALLY, REALLY SIMPLE – DON'T PASS ANYTHING ON**

Put things in perspective

When all is said and done, it is only a job. It ain't your health, your love life, your family, your children, your life or your soul. If, by the way, it is any of these things then you really have gone badly wrong along the way.

Your job is just a job. Yes, I know you need the money etc etc. But it is just a job and there are others.

Having a bad day at work shouldn't cause you to:

- lose sleep
- go off your food
- lose your sex drive
- smoke more
- drink more
- take drugs
- be more irritable
- get depressed
- get stressed.

But you'd be surprised how often these things are done by people because they have had a bad day. Yes, they may have had a whole series of bad days. But taken one by one, it is just a bad day. You have to learn to switch off, relax, not take it so seriously, enjoy it more and put things into perspective.

Get a hobby, get a life. You must work to live, not live to work. Don't take stuff home with you – learn to be assertive and say no. Put your family first. Spend time with your children – they will grow up so fast you will miss their precious childhood if you work your way through it – believe me I have seen my children grow up and it is so swift it is terrifying. It may seem slow and stressful at the time, but it zips past and then is irrecoverably gone – and you missed it because you were doing paperwork of an evening or attending another boring bloody conference at the weekend.

It is just a job.

YOU HAVE TO LEARN TO SWITCH OFF, RELAX, NOT TAKE IT SO SERIOUSLY, ENJOY IT MORE AND PUT THINGS INTO PERSPECTIVE

Never disapprove of others

So, they're all going to the wine bar again this lunchtime. You hate that. You hate the noise, the smell, the inane chatter about last night's TV.

But do you tell them this? No, you do not. You need to be one of the crowd – blend in. You need them to think you're there, in spirit if not in body, without actually being there. Easy. You get out of it by saying you have to do some shopping, visit a friend, go to the gym.

Don't disapprove of the way they spend their lunch break – this will make them think of you as an outsider. Nor do you tell them you're staying in the office to catch up on some work – they will think you a creep. But it is fine to say you are going to do some shopping and then find somewhere nice to park up in your car with a soft drink and a decent sandwich – and your laptop. You can get all that extra work done but you don't have to let them know.

Don't tell them that you think drinking at lunchtime is unhealthy and unproductive – tell them you'll be along in a bit and to carry on without you – 'get one in for me'. This way the lunchtime crowd will accept you as 'one of them' without you ever having to be one. You will be accepted if you don't disapprove.

Or perhaps they all go bowling together on a Tuesday evening. No, you don't say 'but bowling is for geeks, isn't it?' Instead you can say, 'Ah, Tuesday evenings? That's my night for taking my mother to the cinema I'm afraid'. Or how about you swallow your pride, your standards and your disapproval – and actually go. Who knows, maybe you'll have fun. But you will blend in and you won't show that you disapprove of your colleagues. Smart move.

How others spend their leisure time, their money or their lives is no concern of yours. The smart mover concentrates on their own path and ignores the route others choose to take. Keep focused on where you are going and ignore anything others are up to. By ignoring, it is easier to stop making judgements. If you make judgements, you categorise yourself and thus make it much more difficult to be flexible and to move easily from situation to situation. By judging others you, in turn, get pigeon-holed yourself – not a good place to be.

> # THE SMART MOVER CONCENTRATES ON THEIR OWN PATH AND IGNORES THE ROUTE OTHERS CHOOSE TO TAKE

Get people to assume you have already made the step

Act like a general manager and people will accept you as one. Act like an office junior and that's what people will think you are. So how are we going to get people to make this assumption?

- Be confident and assertive and sound mature: 'Yes, we can do that – I'll make sure we get on to that immediately.'

- If you come to work wearing trainers and a track suit, you won't command the same respect as you would if you wore a smart business suit and looked the part.

- Don't talk of 'I' and refer every problem back to how it affects you: 'I can't work through my lunch break, I'm entitled to my hour off' – instead say 'We' and see things from the company's point of view, what's best for the whole organisation: 'We need to pull together here, I'm happy to work through the lunch break to help us get this problem solved.'

- If you talk about what you watched on telly last night and where you are going on holiday and what you are going to do at the weekend, you come across as more lightweight – and thus junior – than if you talked about company issues, what your department's plans are for the future, how the change in interest rates is going to affect business over the next few months and what you are going to do about exchange rates.

Basically, what you have to do is get people to recognise you as a heavyweight and not a lightweight. Be serious, mature, grown up and adult. This doesn't mean you have to be a geek, a nerd, a swot, a goody goody or a bore. You can still take a joke, enjoy a laugh, smile, be light-hearted and jovial, be fun and full of beans. You need to project a mature but fun image. You need to make people aware that you:

- know the job
- are experienced
- are serious
- are reliable and responsible
- are trustworthy
- are in the job you want to be in.

So, take to sauntering around the place looking suave and cool and being very stylish and grown-up, make the appropriate noises and make sure that when you get offered the job you are after, you can already do it.

BE SERIOUS, MATURE, GROWN-UP AND ADULT

THE RULES OF
MANAGEMENT

The Rules of Work was about those Rules that work for you from your very first day, fresh from school, college, training, and go on working for you whatever your role. I'd observed plenty of those in action over my career, so that's what I'd written about. However, there were plenty more Rules that you only really needed to learn once you reached the point where you were leading a team of your own. However if you're following *The Rules of Work* that's likely to be pretty soon, and I could see that I'd need to assemble and write down *The Rules of Management* too.

These Rules seemed to me to fall into two broad categories. Firstly there were the Rules about managing other people. That's the essence of being a manager: you're responsible for other people. Responsible for their work, yes, but also responsible for their motivation, their welfare, their rights and their ability to work with the rest of the team.

You may not have appointed these people. You may not even particularly like them. But it's your job to get the best out of them – as a team, not just as individuals. And there are lots of unspoken Rules for doing just that. Some of them seem obvious as soon as they're pointed out, but if they were that obvious every manager would be following them, and that's certainly not the case. So the first part of *The Rules of Management* sets out these Rules for managing your team.

The second category, and the second section of the book, is about Rules for managing yourself. When you become a manager, suddenly you're supposed to be doing your job *and* worrying about the rest of your team as well. That's a juggling act in itself and, while all the Rules of work still apply, there are suddenly lots of new skills you'll need. But no one is going to tell you what they are. Your bosses might send you on management training workshops and leadership weekends, but there will still be plenty of Rules they don't tell you that the successful managers are all following. So you'd better follow them too.

You're now the filling in a sandwich. You're the buffer between your team, and the higher-ups. You have to explain your team's performance to the bosses, stick up for your department's rights and represent their interests further up the organisation. At the same time, you have to defend to your team the bosses' decision to change working practices or slash budgets or restructure. You have to do this without bad-mouthing either side to the other – you need to keep the respect of both groups, and that is an art you need all the help with that you can get. In other words, you need *The Rules of Management*.

I was interested to see what a wide range of Rules were voted for from this particular book, spread between both sections – Rules for your team and Rules for yourself. Two Rules garnered the most votes: 'Get them emotionally involved' and 'Go home'. It's a rare manager who has ever had either of these Rules spelt out to them in any form of training, and yet every manager needs to know and follow them in order to do their job well.

Get them emotionally involved

You manage people. People who are paid to do a job. But if it is 'just a job' to them, you'll never get their best. If they come to work looking to clock in and clock off and do as little as they can get away with in-between, then you're doomed to failure, my friend. On the other hand, if they come to work looking to enjoy themselves, looking to be stretched, challenged, inspired and to get involved, then you are in with a big chance of getting the very best out of them. Trouble is, the jump from drudge to super team is entirely down to you. It is *you* that has to inspire them, lead them, motivate them, challenge them and get them emotionally involved.

That's OK. You like a challenge yourself, don't you? The good news is that getting a team emotionally involved is easy. All you have to do is make them care about what they are doing. And that's easy too. You have to get them to see the relevance of what they are doing, how it makes an impact on people's lives, how they provide for the needs of other human beings, how they can reach out and touch people by what they do at work. Get them convinced – because it is true of course – that what they do makes a difference, that it contributes to society in some way rather than just lines the owner's or shareholders' pockets, or ensures that the chief executive gets a big fat pay cheque.

And yes, I know it's easier to show how they contribute if you manage nurses rather than an advertising sales team, but if you think about it, then you can find value in any role and instil pride in those who do whatever job it is. Prove it? OK. Well, those who sell advertising space are helping other companies, some of which may be very small, to reach their markets. They are alerting potential customers to things they may have wanted for a long time and may really need. They are keeping the newspaper or magazine afloat – and its staff employed – as it relies on ad sales income, and that magazine or newspaper delivers information and/or gives pleasure to the people who buy it (otherwise they wouldn't, would they?).

Get them to care because that's an easy thing to do. Look, this is a given. Everyone deep down wants to be valued and to be useful. The cynics will say this is nonsense, but it is true, deep down true. All you have to do is reach down far enough and you will find care, feeling, concern, responsibility and involvement. Drag all that stuff up and they'll follow you forever and not even realise why.

Oh, just make sure that you've convinced yourself first before you try this out on your team. Do you believe that what you do makes a positive difference? If you're not sure, reach down, deep down, and find a way of caring ...

> **GET THEM CONVINCED – BECAUSE IT IS TRUE OF COURSE – THAT WHAT THEY DO MAKES A DIFFERENCE**

RULE 2

Accept their limitations

Effectively fusing a team together means you need several different parts – or team members. Now some of us are good at certain things and others not so. If we were all the same we wouldn't be able to work as a team – we would all be leaders or all followers and you need a combination, not either/or.

So if some members of your team aren't leaders – or followers – you have to accept that. If some are good at figure work and others not, you have to accept that. If some are good at working unsupervised and others not, you have to accept that.

And to be able to accept these things you have to know your staff pretty well. You have to know their strengths and weaknesses, good points and bad. If you don't – and I'm sure this doesn't apply to you – you will be forever trying to shove round pegs into square holes and vice versa.

You have to accept that not everyone is going to be as bright, as determined, as ambitious, as clever or as motivated as you are – praise indeed from me, but see the next Rule. Some of your team are quite possibly going to be brain dead from the feet up and you might need to do some judicious pruning[1] if there simply is no hope. But don't act in haste. You might not need a team of geniuses (in fact if you hire people far too smart for a job, they will just leave, fast).

Suppose your team contains machine operators or admin assistants. Now you don't need these good people to have Einstein brains nor to be really on the ball when it comes to brainstorming. But you do need them to be able to sit in an arse-numbing position for hours at a time concentrating on a bit of work that would drive you or me batty. Just don't go expecting them to take creative wing and soar away with new ideas, new innovations or

---

[1] *The Rules of Management* Rule 10: Be ready to prune

new technologies. You have to accept their limitations, and love them for them because these limitations are their parameters by which you can get the very best out of them – their best of course. And while you're at it, have a quick check of your own limitations. What's that? You haven't got any? Come on.

> **IF WE WERE ALL THE SAME WE WOULDN'T BE ABLE TO WORK AS A TEAM – WE WOULD ALL BE LEADERS OR ALL FOLLOWERS**

Encourage people

If you don't let people know you're pleased with them, they'll wilt. People come to work for a whole raft of reasons – most, nothing to do with the money despite what they'll tell you – and right there at the top of their unwritten, unspoken, undeclared list will be 'Praise from the boss'. That's you by the way, the boss.

They might call it 'recognition' or 'acknowledgement' or 'feeling I've done well' – but how do they know? They know because you tell them.

Now you can praise them retroactively, so to speak – wait until they've done good and then tell them they've done good – or you can encourage them in advance – active praise. Tell them they're going to do good before they've done it. Why? Because the chances of them doing good are that much greater if you have praised them in advance. They won't want to let you down, or themselves.

Being a manager is a minimalist's dream. You want to build a great team and you want to do it with the smallest output of resources. Praise is free. It is instantly replaceable, doesn't wear out, is invariably 100 per cent effective, is incredibly simple to do and takes no time at all.

So why don't more managers do it? Because it takes self-assurance. You have to be feeling pretty good about yourself to be able to dish out praise well in advance. If you doubt yourself, you'll doubt them. If you doubt them, you'll not praise them because you'll be sure they are going to screw up.

It takes nothing except courage to say, 'Come on, you can do it. You'll be fine'. The more responsibility you give people, the more you trust them, the more you praise them, the more you encourage them, the more they'll give you in return. Praise costs nothing and brings in loads. Encouragement should be a given.

Encourage an atmosphere where everyone encourages everyone else – 'You can do it' should be heard every day all around you. If you're not saying it, chances are your team isn't either. Encourage the good ones to give the less good ones a hand up. In any good team an air of fostering help should be actively encouraged and praised when it happens. We're all in this together and we sink or swim together.

> # TELL THEM THEY'RE GOING TO DO GOOD BEFORE THEY'VE DONE IT

Be very, very good at finding the right people

You have to be good at finding the right people to fill the right jobs – and then leave them to get on with it. OK, I know this is one rule that requires a certain intuitive touch but I'm sure you know the sort of manager I'm talking about. They seem to surround themselves with capable, competent people and then they just seem to sit back and watch them go for goal. You can do that too. It is a special talent but one you can cultivate. I guess the skill is in both picking the right people *and* letting go – leaving them alone to get on with it. You have to have lots of trust to do that; trust in their ability and trust in your own as well.

You have to have a very clear idea of *who* you are looking for to fill a job as much as *what* you are looking for. For instance, you might need a senior account manager – that is *what* you are looking for. But *who*? Team player? Good all-rounder? Someone able to make decisions on the run? Someone who can plan ahead? Someone who understands your industry's quirks? Someone who speaks fluent spreadsheet? Someone who can work with an over-excitable union?

I'm sure you get the idea. If you have a clear picture of *who* you need as well as *what* you need, you make the transition to being a manager who seems to have an uncanny knack of finding the right people. It's not a knack, of course, but planning, vision, logic and hard work.

I once made the mistake of being totally seduced by a manager's credentials – I was a general manager seeking to employ a manager – and failing to look hard enough at *who* he was rather than *what* he was. Yes, he had the credentials and was very good at his job. But he wasn't a team player and saw everything as a competition, mainly between him and the other managers. Fine in itself, but it didn't work for me or the other managers, who all wanted to pull together. This was one case where I was not good at finding the right person. I had found the wrong person and it took a lot to extricate myself. I had only myself to blame because I hadn't thought sufficiently about who I wanted.

If you're not good at this, or think you could improve, invite somebody you respect to sit in on interviews with you to give you another perspective. Find a mentor or coach to help you work out who you really need.

YOU HAVE TO BE GOOD
AT FINDING THE RIGHT PEOPLE
TO FILL THE RIGHT JOBS – AND
THEN LEAVE THEM TO GET
ON WITH IT

RULE 5

Respect individual differences

I have several children. I expect them to operate as a team. But I am also shrewd enough to realise they are all completely different and if I try to treat them all the same, apply the same rules – apart from the discipline ones – I'll get a mutiny, or chaos. Now one of them – and I'm not mentioning any names here but they will know which one I'm talking about – can't be hurried. Not ever, not anyhow. If you shove, he digs his heels in and can't be shifted. He has to be lured, enticed, seduced into being quicker. But I have another child who constantly has to be slowed down. I have to respect – and work with – their individual differences. I simply have to.

Now your team is just the same. Some members can be hurried and others can't. Some will need to be slowed down and others you need to speed up. Some will come to work with a cheery smile, others are best not approached first thing in the morning. Some will be terribly good with technology and others won't. Look at what Meredith Belbin says about teams[2] and see how everybody in a team has something different to offer – and that difference is what makes your team superb.

With my children if I need something doing fast I know who to call on. If I need a slower, more methodical approach I select another child.

You don't have to let anyone get away with anything just because they are different – keep the discipline rules in place – it's more in the way you treat individual differences, the way you select tasks and the way you expect those tasks to be carried out. We are all

---

[2] *The Rules of Management* Rule 2: Know what a team is and how it works

different, thank God – a world populated by people like me, even I realise, would be ghastly – and those differences are what make a great team pull together effectively.

So if you're managing a sales team, say, and most of the members are sharp-suited and have slick patter (like you), but one prefers casual garb and is more chatty with her customers, don't mark her cards as 'not a company person' – judge her on the results she gets. If she makes her targets and her customers love her, then *vive la différence*.

> # DIFFERENCES ARE WHAT MAKE A GREAT TEAM PULL TOGETHER EFFECTIVELY

Train them to bring you solutions, not problems

It's terribly easy for staff to moan. I think it becomes a habit. You have to train your staff not just to moan. You can allow moaning but insist that if they bring you a problem they must also suggest a solution to the problem. Any idea that there is something wrong should always be met with, 'And what would you like me to do about it?' If they complain, meet them with, 'What do you think we should do?'

The best manager I ever worked for carried this even further and made us tell him the solution first – and then let him guess what he thought our 'problem' was. It made it a game, which was sort of fun, but it also made us think on our feet a bit – made us be a bit lateral in our moaning. I was having a problem with security staff. I thought they were wiping the CCTV footage without watching it, which was not on. This was my problem because if anything had happened I would have carried the can. I needed them to watch carefully but couldn't devise a solution to this problem – but I couldn't just go to the boss and moan that they weren't doing their job properly. I had to come up with a solution first.

Then it dawned on me that I didn't need to go to the boss. I could solve this one myself. I had to make sure the security staff thought there was something worth watching. I mentioned that some members of staff had been reported as having sex somewhere on the premises and it could have been covered by the CCTV cameras, but no one was sure by which camera. There were cameras covering car parks, offices, corridors and storage areas in the basement. Result. The security bods started watching as if their lives depended on it. My boss was pleased because this was part of my job brief and he had noticed it wasn't being done properly and was going to pull me up on it. And I had come up with a solution to a problem without going to my boss and just moaning, 'Oh, the security people aren't doing their job properly ...'

Admittedly I had to come up with a fresh solution once the security staff realised they weren't going to see any smutty pictures – but it took them a long time, and they kept going back just in case ...

ANY IDEA THAT THERE IS SOMETHING WRONG SHOULD ALWAYS BE MET WITH, 'AND WHAT WOULD YOU LIKE ME TO DO ABOUT IT?'

Work hard

The fundamental Rule of management, I'm afraid, is get the basic job done, get it done well and work bloody hard at it. No good being a fantastic people manager if you let the basic job slip. You may have to get into the office earlier than anyone else, earlier than you've ever got there before, but get in early you must.

Once you have cleared your work out of the way you can concentrate on managing your team. Paperwork has to be done efficiently and on time. This isn't the place to go into lengthy training sessions on time management and the like, but basically you will have to be:

- organised
- dedicated
- ruthlessly efficient
- focused.

No choice, I'm afraid. You have to knuckle down and get on with it. Management isn't swanning around issuing orders and looking cool. It's actually about what goes on in the background – the work being done where no one sees it. And if you're going to achieve that without spending unnecessary time on it, you'll have to learn those basic organisational skills.

And if you want to know if you are being a good manager now – take a look at your desk. Go on. Right now. What do you see? Clear space and order? Paper everywhere and piles of unsorted stuff? Do the same with your briefcase, files, computer even. Order or disorder?

You have to use whatever tools you have to hand to make sure the work is done, done well, and done on time. Make lists, use pop-up calendars on your computer, delegate, seek help, stay up late, get up early, get up earlier. Obviously you still need to refer to Rule 10: Go home – you have to have a life. But get that work done and learn to be ruthlessly efficient.

> ## YOU HAVE TO KNUCKLE
> ## DOWN AND GET ON WITH IT

Be proactive, not reactive

I know, I know, it takes you all your time just to get the job done, the paperwork tidied and the plants watered without having to think about the future or be a whiz innovator. But the smart manager – that's you again – puts aside 30 minutes a week for forward planning. Try asking yourself simple questions: 'How can I generate more sales?' 'What can I do more expediently?' 'How could I cut staff turnover?' 'How can I convert more leads to sales?' 'How could I streamline the accounting procedure?' 'How could I move into another sector?' 'How could I get my team to work harder, faster, brighter?' 'How could I get them to brainstorm more freely?' 'How could I hold meetings that wouldn't waste so much time?'

There is an old saying, 'If you always do what you've always done, you'll always get what you've always got'. And by golly it's true. If you aren't proactive you'll stagnate. And if you do that, the crocodiles will bite your bum. You have to keep paddling, keep moving forwards in the water. Sharks have to keep moving forwards all their life to keep water passing through or over their gills. They never stop. Be a shark. Keep moving forwards. Because if you don't there will be plenty of others willing to do so.

And believe me, I know what it's like. You open your inbox and there are loads of emails to deal with. Then there's the paperwork. Then there are the staff issues. Then there's lunch. Then there's the afternoon work to be done and then there's a panic to get all the latest urgent emails dealt with and then there's a quick cup of tea and then it's about time to pack it all in and go home and there's this idiot telling me I've got to take 30 minutes out of a jam-packed day to think about the future. Yeah, in your dreams.

But those 30 minutes can be combined with another task. Once a week I have lunch on my own and spend the time being proactive, thinking about the future, thinking of ways to be one jump ahead of the competition. But I do have to go out alone for that lunch or people come and interrupt my mental planning session.

BE A SHARK. KEEP
MOVING FORWARDS

Have principles and stick to them

When you think about it, you've got to have principles. If you don't, you end up despising yourself or in debt or in prison. You might end up like this anyway, but at least you could say, 'I have my principles'.

There has to be a line beyond which you will not go. You have to know where that line is drawn. No one else has to know until they ask you to cross it and then you can tell them. That line has to be a 10-mile-high solid steel wall. You can't go beyond it, no matter what.

I have a friend whose boss once asked her to falsify a formal warning letter to present at a tribunal for a member of staff who had been sacked and was claiming unfair dismissal. Would you do this? Does it matter whether you think the person was rightly or wrongly dismissed? Suppose they *had* been warned but it hadn't been recorded in writing? Suppose you and your boss were sure it must have been put in writing at the time, but you can't find it now? I'm not telling you what's right or wrong in this instance. I'm saying that *you* have to know what *you* consider to be right or wrong. And then stand by it.

So where would you draw your line? I've been asked to do things I didn't like. I've been asked to do things I found unpleasant. I've been asked to do things I found extremely irksome, but whenever I've been asked to cross my own personal line – which thankfully in a long business career has been only once or twice – I was able to say no, and stick to it. And each time I got a pat on the back rather than a trip to the Job Centre.

THERE HAS TO BE A LINE
BEYOND WHICH YOU WILL
NOT GO. YOU HAVE TO KNOW
WHERE THAT LINE IS DRAWN

Go home

One manager I worked with stayed late, got in early, skipped lunch and kept his head down and grafted every second he was there. Guess who got promoted over him? My boss Bob, who didn't do any of those things.

One of Bob's favourite lines, to me anyway, was, 'Go home, Rich, go home. You've got a young family, go home and see them before they forget what you look like. Either that or send them a photo before they really forget'. Naturally I went home. As did Bob, a lot. In fact he was at work so little he got promoted again.

His secret? His team, of which I was one, would have done anything for him. We went that extra mile. We would never have willingly let him down. Bob inspired loyalty in his staff in a way I've rarely seen since. He made all of us feel grown-up, trusted, treated in a respectful way. He never shouted, abused, put upon, demanded, overworked, or humiliated his team. I never saw him have to discipline anyone, ever. He was charismatic and charming, cool and relaxed. He cooked us all like small fish.

He said his secret was his family. For them he worked. He adored his children and would rather have been home with them than working. His love for them showed and he wore the badge of happy family man with great pride. He talked a lot about his kids and his wife and was obviously very happy with them.

He never stayed late because that would have been disloyal to his number-one priority – his family. This gave him great depth. He was well rounded and balanced. He was at ease with himself. He had nothing to prove at work because he was content at home. I've worked with some complete bastards and I can say the only thing they all had in common was a bad home life. Their base camp was corrupt and it showed. So, my dear friend, go home.

HE HAD NOTHING TO PROVE
AT WORK BECAUSE HE WAS
CONTENT AT HOME

THE RULES OF
LIFE

Once I got into the habit of recording the Rules of work and management, it became pretty obvious that these kinds of Rules apply to all areas of life, and not just from 9 to 5. My publisher and I started talking about expanding them beyond the workplace, and before long I'd put together *The Rules of Life*. It's been the most successful of all the books in the series, presumably because its scope applies to absolutely all of us.

Of course there are more than 100 Rules worth following over a lifetime, but I set out to encapsulate the most important ones as I saw them. In other words the Rules I'd most often seen used by people who were happy and successful. As with all the books, these weren't necessarily Rules that I managed to follow all the time myself, but they were ones which I could see worked, and which I certainly tried to follow – and generally regretted when I didn't[3].

As I began assembling this set of Rules, I could see that they fell into four broad categories:

- Rules for you
- Partnership Rules
- Family and friends Rules
- Social Rules.

The first section was about your own attitudes and mind-sets, and the other three sections covered Rules for interacting with other people, starting with your partner and

---

[3] Personally I tend to struggle most with the Rules that require patience or restraint.

then spreading out to family, friends and your wider social circle. A lot of the later books expanded on some of these areas, for example *The Rules of People*. The later books come at these from a different angle, with greater focus to these more specific areas, although of course there's the occasional overlap (it would be weird if there wasn't). However, *The Rules of Life* still gives the broadest picture of these absolutely essential Rules for getting through life as enjoyably as possible.

So *The Rules of Life* was one of the earliest books in the series, it deals with – well, the whole of life – and is widely available worldwide. No surprise then that overall it received more votes for individual Rules than any of the other books. As a result, I have to tell you that many of the Rules that collected a high number of votes still didn't make it into the top 10 here. Honourable mentions have to go to 'Change what you can change and let go of the rest', 'Leave a little space for yourself each day', and 'Only dead fish swim with the stream'.

I haven't particularly set out the Rules in each section of this book according to the largest number of nominations; however, in this section the first three Rules are the ones that were most voted for.

Keep it under your hat

You are about to become a Rules Player. You are about to embark on a life-changing adventure, possibly, if you choose to accept your mission. You are about to discover ways to become positive, happier and more successful in everything you do. So there's no need to say anything to anybody about it. Keep quiet. No one likes a smart arse. That's it. First Rule: *keep it under your hat.*

There may well be times when you do want to talk to other people about what you're doing because, quite naturally, you want to share it with somebody. Well, you can't and you don't. Let them find out for themselves with no clues from you. You may think this unfair but it is actually fairer than you believe. If you tell them, they'll shy away. And quite rightly so – we all hate being preached at. It's a bit like when you give up smoking and suddenly find this new healthier way of living and you simply have to convert all your old smoking friends. Trouble is, they aren't ready to quit yet and you find they label you as smug or a prig or, even worse, an ex-smoker. And how we all hate those.

So the first Rule is, quite simply, don't preach, propagate, try to convert, shout from the rooftops or even mention this.

You will get a warm glow from changing your attitude to life and having people ask what it is you have done, are doing, and you can say that it's nothing, merely a sunny day and you feel better/happier/livelier/jollier/whatever. There is no need to go into any detail because that's not really what people want to know. In fact it's exactly the opposite of what they want to know. It's a bit like when someone asks how you are. What they really want to hear is just the one word, 'Fine'. Even if you are in the very pits of despair, that's all they want to hear because anything more requires commitment on their part. And for a casual 'How are you?' that's most certainly not what they want. What they want is just 'Fine'. And then they can be about their business without any further involvement. If you don't say 'Fine', but instead unburden yourself, they will back off pretty quickly.

And it's the same with being a Rules Player. No one really wants to know, so keep quiet. How do I know? Because when I wrote *The Rules of Work*, which turned a lot of people on to the ability to be successful in the workplace without having to resort to underhand means, I suggested the same thing and found it worked. Just get on with it, do it quietly and go about your daily life happily and smugly without having to tell anyone anything.

> # DON'T PREACH, PROPAGATE
> # OR TRY TO CONVERT

You'll get older but not necessarily wiser

There is an assumption that as we get older we will get wiser; not true I'm afraid. The rule is we carry on being just as daft, still making plenty of mistakes. It's just that we make new ones, different ones. We do learn from experience and may not make the same mistakes again, but there is a whole new pickle jar of fresh ones just lying in wait for us to trip up and fall into. The secret is to accept this and not to beat yourself up when you do make new ones. The Rule really is: be kind to yourself when you do muck things up. Be forgiving and accept that it's all part of that growing older but no wiser routine.

Looking back, we can always see the mistakes we made, but we fail to see the ones looming up. Wisdom isn't about not making mistakes, but about learning to escape afterwards with our dignity and sanity intact.

When we are young, ageing seems to be something that happens to, well, old people. But it does happen to us all and we have no choice but to embrace it and roll with it. Whatever we do and whoever we are, the fact is we are going to get older. And this ageing process does seem to speed up as we get older.

You can look at it this way – the older you get, the more areas you've covered to make mistakes in. There will always be new areas of experience where we have no guidelines and where we'll handle things badly, overreact, get it wrong. And the more flexible we are, the more adventurous, the more life-embracing, then the more new avenues there will be to explore – and make mistakes in of course.

As long as we look back and see where we went wrong and resolve not to repeat such mistakes, there is little else we need to do. Remember that any Rules that apply to you also apply to everyone else around you. They are all getting older too. And not any wiser particularly. Once you accept this, you'll be more forgiving and kinder towards yourself and others.

Finally, yes, time does heal and things do get better as you get older. After all, the more mistakes you've made, the less likely that you'll come up with new ones. The best thing is that if you get a lot of your mistakes over and done with early on in life, there will be less to learn the hard way later on. And that's what youth is all about, a chance to make all the mistakes you can and get them out of the way.

WISDOM ISN'T ABOUT NOT MAKING MISTAKES BUT ABOUT LEARNING TO ESCAPE AFTERWARDS WITH OUR DIGNITY AND SANITY INTACT

Accept yourself

If you accept that what's done is done, you are left with yourself exactly as you are. You can't go back and change anything, so you've got to work with what you've got. I'm not suggesting anything New Age here such as love yourself – that's far too ambitious. No, let's begin with simple accepting. Accepting is easy because it is exactly what it says – accepting. You don't have to improve or change or strive for perfection. Quite the opposite. Just accept.

That means accepting all the warts and emotional lumps and bumps, the bad bits, the weaknesses and the rest of it. This doesn't mean we are happy with everything about ourselves, or that we are going to be lazy and lead a bad life. We are going to accept the way we are, initially, and then build on that. What we are *not* going to do is beat ourselves up because we don't like some bits. Yes, we can change lots but that will come later. We're only up to Rule 3 here.

This has to be a Rule because there can be no choice here. We have to accept that we are the way we are – the result of everything that has happened. It all just is. You, like me, like all of us, are human. That means you're pretty complex. You come fully loaded with desires, anguish, sins, pettiness at times, mistakes, ill temper, rudeness, deviation, hesitation and repetition. That's what makes a human being so wonderful, the complexity.

None of us can ever be perfect. We start with what we've got and who we are, and then we can only make a choice, each day, to strive for some kind of better. And that's all we can ask of ourselves – to make that choice. To be awake and aware, to be ready to do the right thing. And accept that some days you aren't going to make it. Some days you will, like all of us, fall far short. That's OK, don't beat yourself up. Pick yourself up and start again. Accept that you will fail from time to time and that you are human.

I know it can be hard at times, but once you have picked up the gauntlet of becoming a Rules Player, you're well on the path to improvement. Stop picking faults with yourself, or giving yourself a hard time. Instead, accept that you are what you are. You're doing the best you can at this point in time, so give yourself a pat on the back and press on.

> YOU DON'T HAVE TO IMPROVE
> OR CHANGE OR STRIVE FOR
> PERFECTION. QUITE THE
> OPPOSITE. JUST ACCEPT

RULE 4

Dedicate your life to something

To know what counts and what doesn't, you have to know what you are dedicating your life to. There are, of course, no right or wrong answers to this one as it's a very personal choice – but it's really useful to have an answer, rather than not really knowing.

As an example, my own life has been driven by two things: (a) someone once told me that if my soul or spirit was the only thing I was likely to be taking with me when I went, then it ought to be the best thing I had; (b) my curious upbringing.

The first one isn't, for me at least, in any way religious. It just struck a chord with me, triggered something. Whatever it was I was taking with me, then perhaps I ought to do a bit of work on it. Make sure it really is the very best thing about me. That got me thinking. How on earth do you go about that? The answer still is that I haven't got a clue. I have explored and experimented, learned and made mistakes, been a seeker and a follower, read and observed and wrestled with this great problem all my life. How do you go about improving your life on that level? I think the only conclusion I have come to is to live as decent a life as possible, to go through causing as little damage as possible, to treat everyone with whom I come into contact with respect and dignity. It's something to dedicate my life to and it works for me.

And how can my curious upbringing cause me to focus on what I am dedicating my life to? Well, having had a 'dysfunctional' upbringing and having chosen to let it motivate me rather than affect me, I am acutely aware that many people also need to throw off that feeling of being badly affected by what has gone before. This is what I dedicate my life to. Yes, it might be crazy; *I* might be crazy. But at least I have something I can focus on, something (for me) that counts.

Now none of this is big stuff and by that I mean I don't go around with this emblazoned on my forehead – 'Templar dedicates his life to ...' sort of thing. It's more that, quietly, in my heart, I have something that I can devote my attention to. It's a yardstick by which I can measure (a) how I'm doing, (b) what I'm doing and (c) where I'm going. You don't need to trumpet it. You don't need to tell anyone (see Rule 1). You don't even need to think it out in too much detail. A simple internal mission statement will do. Decide what it is you are dedicating your life to. It makes the rest much easier.

A SIMPLE INTERNAL MISSION STATEMENT WILL DO

No fear, no surprise, no hesitation, no doubt

Where does this come from? It's from a seventeenth-century samurai warrior. This was his four-point key to successful living – and swordsmanship.

- **No fear.** There should be nothing in this life that you are afraid of. If there is, you might need to do some work on overcoming that fear. Here I have to confess to a certain fear of heights. I avoid high places if I can. Recently, owing to leaky gutters, I had to crawl out on our roof – three floors up with a very long drop on one side. I gritted my teeth and kept repeating, 'No fear, no fear, no fear', until the job was done. Oh yes, and of course I didn't look down. Whatever your fear, face it head on and defeat it.

- **No surprise.** Life seems to be full of them, doesn't it? You're going along swimmingly and suddenly something huge rears up ahead of you. But if you look carefully, there were clues all along the way that it was going to happen. No surprise there then. Whatever your situation now, it is going to change. No surprises there. So why does life seem to surprise us then? Because we are asleep half the time. Wake up and nothing can sneak up on you.

- **No hesitation.** Weigh up the odds and then just get on with it. If you hang back, the opportunity will have passed. If you spend too long thinking, you'll never make a move. Once we have looked at the options, we make a choice, a decision and then go for it. That's the secret. No hesitation means not waiting around for other people to help out or make up our minds for us. No hesitation means if there is a certain inevitability about a situation then just throw yourself in head first and enjoy the ride. If there is nothing to be done then waiting doesn't help.

- **No doubt.** Once you have made up your mind about something, don't go over it again and again. Stop thinking and enjoy – relax and let go. Stop worrying. Tomorrow will come along as certainly as it can. There is no doubt about life. It just is. Be confident. Be committed. Be sure of yourself. Once you have committed yourself to a set course, a path, a plan, then follow it through. Have no doubt it was the right thing to do and no doubt that you will succeed. Get on with it and trust your judgement completely.

> # WAKE UP AND NOTHING
> # CAN SNEAK UP ON YOU

It's OK to give up

You know how you sometimes hear stories about people who have failed their driving test 35 times? Much as you admire their persistence, don't you sometimes wonder why they don't just give up? These are clearly people who just aren't cut out to drive big, heavy, dangerous lumps of machinery around streets full of children, old people, dogs and lamp posts. Even if they do finally pass, there's a feeling that it's probably a fluke, and you probably still wouldn't want to be a passenger on their next trip.

Actually, if these people held their hands up (as some do) and said, 'You know what? This isn't me. I'm going to get a bicycle and a bus season ticket', I would applaud their ability to see what was staring them in the face. I wouldn't call them quitters, or criticise their lack of determination or drive.[4] They'd simply be getting the message loud and clear, and having the good sense not to ignore it.

Sometimes we head off down the wrong path in life, often with the best motives. Maybe there's no knowing it's the wrong path until we try it. There's no shame in admitting it once we realise it's not getting us where we want to be. When you realise this college course isn't right for you, or that you don't have what it takes to do this job well, or that your move to a new city isn't working out, or that the hours you put into being on the local council put too much strain on your family, it takes guts to say so. That's not quitting. That's courage.

Quitting is when you give up because you don't want to put in the effort, you can't be bothered, you don't like hard work, you're scared of failure. We Rules Players don't quit. We harden our resolve and we get on with the job without complaint.

---

[4] Sorry, couldn't resist that one.

However, a good Rules Player knows when they're beat. If the world is telling you that you took a wrong turning, you can admit it honestly and put yourself on a different track. No one can be brilliant at everything, and sometimes you have to try things to find out whether you can do them. And maybe you can't.

A few years ago a leading UK government minister resigned from her post, famously saying that she was simply 'not up to the job'. Now, I'd never really rated her up to that point, but she rose hugely in my estimation – and that of many others – for that admission. That took guts. Maybe she wasn't great at leading a government department, but she was certainly in a different league from most politicians when it comes to honesty, courage and self-knowledge. She's an outstanding example of the fact that if you give up in the right way at the right time, you're showing strength of character, not weakness.

> # A GOOD RULES PLAYER
> # KNOWS WHEN THEY'RE BEAT

Don't dwell on the past

Whatever the past was, it's gone. There is nothing you can do to change anything that has gone before and so you must turn your attention to the here and now. It is hard to resist the allure of dwelling on what has gone before. But if you want to be successful in your life, you have to turn your attention to what is happening for you right now. You might be tempted to dwell on the past because it was awful or because it was wonderful. Either way, you have to leave it behind because the only way to live is in the present.

If you're revisiting the past because of regrets, then you need to be clear that you can't go back and undo what you've done. If you hang on to guilt, you're only damaging yourself. We've all made bad decisions that have adversely affected people around us that we professed to love but whom we treated disgracefully. There isn't anything you can do to wipe the slate clean. What you can do is to resolve not to make such bad decisions again. That's all anyone can ask of us – that we acknowledge where we messed up and are trying our hardest not to repeat the pattern.

If the past was better for you and you hanker after your glory days, then learn to appreciate the memories but also move on and put your efforts into finding a different kind of good time right now. If it truly was better back then (take off those rose-tinted spectacles for a minute), maybe you can analyse exactly why – money, power, health, vitality, fun, youth. Then move on to find other avenues to explore. We all have to leave good stuff behind and find new challenges, new areas to inspire us.

Every day that we wake up to is a fresh start and we can make of it what we want, write what we want on that blank canvas. Keeping that enthusiasm going can be tough – a bit like trying to take up exercise. The first few times are impossibly hard but if you persevere then one day you find you're jogging, walking, swimming without conscious effort. But getting going is really tough and requires immense powers of concentration, enthusiasm, dedication and perseverance to keep at it.

Try to see the past as a room separate from the one you live in now. You can go in there but you don't live there any more. You can go visit but it isn't home any more. Home is here now. Each second of this present is precious. Don't waste any drops of precious time by spending too much time in that old room. Don't miss what is happening now because you were too busy looking back, or later you'll be busy looking back at this time and wondering why you wasted it. Live here, live now, live in this moment.

> LIVE HERE, LIVE NOW, LIVE IN
> THIS MOMENT

You'll never understand everything

Look, we are tiny complex humans in a huge complex world (and even bigger universe). It's all so unimaginably, fantastically strange that, believe me, we'll never be able to understand everything. And that applies at all levels and in all areas of life. Once you grasp this Rule you'll sleep easier at night.

There are likely to be a few things going on around you right now, as there always will be, that will remain just slightly outside your comprehension. People will behave oddly and you won't understand why. Things will go unexpectedly wrong – or right – and it won't make sense. Spend all your time desperately trying to work it all out and you'll drive yourself crazy. Much better just to accept that there is always stuff that we won't understand and let it go at that. How simple that is.

It's the same principle for the big stuff – why things happen to us, why we are here, where we go afterwards, that sort of thing. Some of it we'll never know, some of it we can try and work out, but I have a sneaking feeling it won't turn out to be anything like we think.

It's as if our lives are an enormous jigsaw and all we get access to is the bottom left-hand bit. And from that we make these huge assumptions: 'Oh, it's a . . . ' But when the veil gets taken away we see that the jigsaw is massive and that the one tiny bit we were scrutinising was actually something else, and there we are looking at an entirely different picture to the one we'd imagined.

We are now collecting information faster than any human, or any computer, can process it. We can't understand it all. We can't even begin to understand a tiny fraction of it. Same with our lives. Stuff is going on around us at such a rate we'll never get to the bottom of it. Because as fast as we try, the picture changes, new information comes in and our understanding alters.

Be curious, ask questions, wonder to yourself, talk to other people if you like – but know that this won't always give you a clear and concrete answer. People don't always make sense. Life doesn't always make sense. Let it go and discover the peace of mind that comes with knowing that you'll never understand everything. Sometimes it just is.

> PEOPLE WILL BEHAVE
> ODDLY. THINGS WILL GO
> UNEXPECTEDLY WRONG –
> OR RIGHT

RULE 9

Know when to let go – when to walk away

Sometimes you have to just walk away. We all hate to fail, hate to give up, hate to give in. We love the challenge of life and want to keep on until whatever we are trying to 'win' has been overcome, vanquished, beaten, won. But sometimes it just ain't going to happen and we need to learn to recognise those moments, learn how to shrug philosophically and walk away with our pride intact and our dignity high.

Sometimes you really want to do something, but it is unrealistic. Instead of knocking yourself out, cultivate the art of knowing when to walk away and you'll find it a lot less stressful.

If a relationship is coming to its end, instead of playing out long and complicated – and potentially hurtful – end games, learn the art of walking away. If it's dead, leave it. This Rule isn't in the partnership section – it's here because it is for you, to protect you, to nurture you. This is nothing to do with 'them' but all to do with you. If it's dead, don't go digging it up every five minutes to check if there's a pulse. It's dead, walk away.

You may want to get even – don't get mad, walk away. This is much better than getting even because it shows you have risen above whatever it is that is driving you crazy. And there can be no better way of getting even than to ignore something so completely it can be left behind.

Letting go and walking away means you are exercising control and good decision-making powers – you are making your choice rather than letting the situation control you.

I don't want to be rude but your problems – hey, my problems too – won't even warrant a footnote in the history of the universe. Walk away now and look back after ten years and I bet you'll be hard pushed to even remember what it was all about. No, this isn't a 'time is the best healer' crusade, but putting space and time between you and your troubles does give you a wider view, a better perspective. And the way to do that is to walk away, put that space there. Time will put itself there, in time of course.

> IF IT'S DEAD, DON'T
> GO DIGGING IT UP EVERY
> FIVE MINUTES TO CHECK
> IF THERE'S A PULSE. IT'S
> DEAD, WALK AWAY

Find a new rule every day – or occasionally at least

So, in *The Rules of Life* you have 100 or so Rules for a successful and fulfilled life. Phew. But don't think it's over. There is no time to sit still, there are no tea breaks for Rules Players. As soon as you think you've got it sussed, you'll fall flat on your face. You have to keep moving forwards. You have to be inventive, creative, imaginative, resourceful and original. This final Rule has to be to keep thinking up new Rules, not to stand still, to carry on developing this theme, adding to, improving on, evolving and growing and changing these Rules. These provide a jumping-off point. They're not a revelation, more a reminder. These Rules are a starting point for you to pick up and run with.

I've tried to avoid the pedestrian ('Time is a great healer') and the humorous ('Never tip anyone who isn't looking') and the impractical ('Love everyone'), the plain daft ('Turn the other cheek' – you get hit twice that way, better to run I say), the wibbly ('Everyone's a rainbow'), the obviously wrong ('There are no victims') and the very, very difficult ('Spend 35 years in a cave and you'll find the secret of the universe' – and get a wet bottom). I've also avoided the trite ('It'll be alright on the night' – my experience is it never is) and the unpleasant ('Don't get mad, get even').

I hope you too will follow a similar plan when you formulate new Rules for yourself. I guess the main thing is that you need to continually formulate your own Rules. When you learn something – from observation or just an illuminating moment – absorb the lesson and see if there's a Rule there for future use.

Try to find a new Rule every day – or at least occasionally. And I am quite genuine about wanting to know what you come up with

– if you want to share them. Being a Rules Player is a lot of fun and it is quite fascinating to try and spot other Players. Whatever you do though, don't go telling everyone about it. Keep it secret, keep it safe – but you can tell me at www.facebook.com/richardtemplar

Being a Rules Player requires dedication, hard work, perseverance, keenness, ambition, enthusiasm, devotion and sheer doggedness. Keep at it and you will live a fulfilled, happy and productive life. But go easy on yourself, we all fail from time to time and no one is perfect – I'm most certainly not. Enjoy and have fun and be good.

> # THESE RULES ARE A REMINDER. THEY ARE A STARTING POINT FOR YOU TO PICK UP AND RUN WITH

THE RULES OF
WEALTH

I could tell from the correspondence I was getting about the first three books in the series that a lot of readers wanted to know how to be more financially successful. From readers stuck in the poverty trap, to those who were comfortable but wanted more – for security, or to be able to splash out, or perhaps for a specific large purchase, or to help support their wider family, or maybe just so they could stop worrying.

Of course there are plenty of books out there that will give you advice – often very good advice – on how to turn what money you have into more money. However the principle behind the Rules is a bit different, as you'll realise. It's not about practical tips and advice – which I'm certainly not particularly qualified to give when it comes to stocks and shares, investments, or many other financial schemes. The Rules are about you, your mindset and attitudes, and I'd certainly noticed plenty of those when observing the wealthiest people I'd encountered during my life.

I'd already noted down plenty of these informally, and I was getting better all the time at identifying Rules. I'd always observed people of course, and thought about what made them tick – lots of us do that and I'm certainly a keen people-watcher – and it turns out that the more you train yourself to extract the underlying Rule from what you're seeing, the easier it becomes to spot them.

The Rules of Wealth divided themselves into five sections when I started to write the book:

- Thinking wealthy
- Getting wealthy

- Getting even wealthier

- Staying wealthy

- Sharing your wealth.

I included this last section because I'd noticed that the rich people who didn't share at least some of their wealth didn't seem to gain as much satisfaction from it as those who did. There are lots of ways to share what you have, and plenty of people to share it with, so I wanted to pass on the principles that seemed to work for the wealthiest people I knew.

I was extremely pleased to discover that the most popular Rule in the book was 'Anybody can be wealthy – you just need to apply yourself'. I hate to see people trapped in a pit – financial or otherwise – and feeling that it's not an option to climb out of it. So it was good to see how many people had taken on board that when it comes to money, you can always improve your lot. The Rules that follow are the most popular ones that will help you do just that.

Anybody can be wealthy – you just need to apply yourself

The lovely thing about money is that it really doesn't discriminate. It doesn't care what colour or race you are, what class you are, what your parents did, or even who you *think* you are. Each and every day starts with a clean slate so that no matter what you did yesterday, today begins anew and you have the same rights and opportunities as everyone else to take as much as you want. The only thing that can hold you back is yourself and your own money myths.[5]

Of the wealth of the world each has as much as they take. What else could make sense? There is no way money can know who is handling it, what their qualifications are, what ambitions they have or what class they belong to. Money has no ears or eyes or senses. It is inert, inanimate, impassive. It hasn't a clue. It is there to be used and spent, saved and invested, fought over, seduced with and worked for. It has no discriminatory apparatus so it can't judge whether you are 'worthy' or not.

I have watched a lot of extremely wealthy people and the one thing they all have in common is that they have nothing in common – apart from all being Rules Players of course. The wealthy are a diverse band of people – the least likely can be loaded. They vary from the genteel to the uncouth, the savvy to the plain stupid, the deserving to the undeserving. But each and every one of them has stepped up and said, 'Yes please, I want some of that'. And the poor are the ones saying, 'No thank you, not for me, I

---

[5] See *The Rules of Wealth* Rule 7: Understand your money beliefs and where they come from

am not worthy. I am not deserving enough. I couldn't. I mustn't. I shouldn't'.

That's what this book is about – challenging your perceptions of money and the wealthy. We all assume the poor are poor because of circumstances, their background, their upbringing, their nurture. But if you have the means to buy a book such as this and live in comparative security and comfort in the world then you too have the power to be wealthy. It may be hard. It may be tough but it is doable. And that is Rule 1 – anyone can be wealthy, you just need to apply yourself. All the other Rules are about that application.

> # YOU HAVE THE SAME RIGHTS AND OPPORTUNITIES AS EVERYONE ELSE TO TAKE AS MUCH AS YOU WANT

Decide on your definition of wealth

So what, to *you*, is wealth? This is one question you have to sit down and work out in advance if you are going to get wealthy. My observation is that wealthy people invariably have worked this one out. They know exactly what, to them, wealth means.

I have a wealthy and extremely generous friend who says that he knew long ago when he was starting out in business that he would consider he had made enough when he wasn't living off the money he had amassed (which we will call his capital). Nor would he be living off the interest on his capital. No, he would consider himself wealthy when he was living on the interest on the interest on his capital. Sounds good to me.

Now, this friend knows how much his interest on the interest is making him, pretty much by the hour. Thus if we all go out for a meal in the evening he knows (a) how much the meal has cost and (b) how much he has made while eating the meal. He says that as long as (b) is more than (a), he is happy.

This is setting the definition of wealth pretty high, you might think. Maybe you wouldn't want to set it this high. And that's fine of course. Then again, maybe you'd want to put some kind of figure on it. In the old days everyone wanted to be a millionaire. That was an easy one to judge if you'd got there or not. Today there are a lot of people who have houses worth more than that and they wouldn't consider themselves wealthy at all and yet haven't quite got around to upping the ante to wishing themselves billionaires.[6]

My own definition, for comparison, is having enough so that I don't have to worry about having enough. How much is that? I

---

[6] Sorry, but to me a billion is a million million and I won't be persuaded otherwise.

never know. There always seems to be more to worry about – and less coming in. But seriously, I feel that I have been 'comfortable' since I started counting in thousands rather than in pounds. I know to the nearest thousand how much I've got, how much I need and how much I can spend.

For some people, not worrying might mean having enough to pay for any emergency that might arise in their family or home. So how will you define it? By the number of cars you own? Servants? Cash in the bank? Value of your house? Portfolio of investments? There are, of course, no right or wrong answers, but I do feel that until you've worked this one out you shouldn't read on. If we don't have a target we can't take aim. If we don't have a destination we can't leave home or we'll be driving around in circles for hours. If we don't have a definition how can we monitor or judge success? If we don't do this how will you know if this book has been helpful to you?

> **IF WE DON'T HAVE A DEFINITION HOW CAN WE MONITOR OR JUDGE SUCCESS? IF WE DON'T DO THIS HOW WILL YOU KNOW IF THIS BOOK HAS BEEN HELPFUL TO YOU?**

Most people are too lazy to be wealthy

You have to get up early, work hard all day and go to bed still working on your objective. Yes, money *does* sometimes grow on trees – or so it seems. Yes, people *do* win the lottery, the jackpot, the big prize. People *do* get sudden inheritances from long lost relatives. Yes, people *do* suddenly find fame and fortune where they sought for none. But it isn't going to happen to you. Well, the odds are that it won't. If you set your objective as 'Win the lottery and live in the lap of luxury for ever more', then read no further. Put this book down and go and buy lottery tickets. If your objective is a little more realistic then read on.

Most people are too lazy to be rich. They may say they want to be, but they don't. They may buy a lottery ticket as a sort of half-hearted gesture of wanting to be rich, but they aren't prepared to put in the work. They aren't prepared to make sacrifices, study, learn, work their socks off, put in the effort and make it a determined and concentrated focus of their life.

And for a lot of them – not you – it is because they believe that if you do so you are somehow tainted with evil[7]. But is it OK to work hard to make money? Is it a worthwhile thing to want? It depends on why and what you are going to do with it I guess.

Most people don't want to do the work. Yes, they want the money but only if it comes to them by accident, by luck, by chance. Then it's OK. Then it's not tainted with sweat and work and passion and focus.

I think if you look at anyone rich enough to be a role model – Bill Gates, Richard Branson, Warren Buffett, James Dyson, Elon Musk,

---

[7] *The Rules of Wealth* Rule 7 (again): Understand your money beliefs and where they come from

Petr Kellner[8] – you'll notice only one thing in common . . . they work their socks off. They might make their money from computers, sales, business, the film industry, vacuum cleaners, pop music, radio stations, cars, whatever. But the one thing they all share is the ability to do more in a day than most of us do in a month.

And that's the wonderful thing about wealth – it's lying around waiting to be claimed (remember Rule 1). And those who claim it are the ones who get up early, work hard and put in the hours.

And you are going to have to as well. I don't have loungers, weight shifters or decorative spongers on my team. I want hard-working, dedicated, focused, ambitious, driven money-makers. With a sense of fun of course.

> # MOST PEOPLE ARE TOO LAZY TO BE RICH. THEY MAY SAY THEY WANT TO BE, BUT THEY DON'T

---

[8] I did have a bet with myself that you wouldn't have heard of him – the Czech Republic's first billionaire.

Decide what you want money for

This is part of your defining, setting an objective process. There are no right or wrong answers. For example, making a fortune and spending it all on cocaine seems, to me, like a foolish thing to do. But that's personal. You might find a problem with me spending mine on a decent Châteauneuf-du-Pape. We all spend on what we think will satisfy us, make us happy. We all choose our own pleasures and it's not for me to sit in judgement on anyone else.

So why do you want to be wealthy? The answers you give will tell you a whole lot about your hidden money myths and how you really see money.

Sometimes it's very simple: we have a dream and need the money to fulfil it. The dream comes first. Gerald Durrell had wanted a zoo since he was a small boy and wrote 36 best-selling books which helped to fund his zoo (on the island of Jersey). What's your dream?

It might not be that simple, however. I asked a close acquaintance why she wanted to be wealthier the other day and the results were quite revealing. She said she wanted to be 'better off' so that she could give her children more. And in giving them more, they would stay at home longer. And if they stayed at home longer, she wouldn't have to face a possible old age alone. So basically she wants to be wealthy to stave off loneliness. Another acquaintance said he wanted to get wealthy so he could have adventures. When pressed further it seemed his adventures were the 'running away' sort where he could be young, free and single again. Is money really the answer for either of these people? Is it for you?

When you know what you want greater wealth for, think also about alternative ways to meet your needs: I said earlier some people want to be wealthy so they can pay for medical care for any close family member that might need it. They could invest in some simple medical insurance to cover that instead.

Consider also what you *don't* need more money for. I like my toys – cars and boats – but have found that my investments in such things hasn't increased as my income has gone up. I still like old cheap sports cars and old boats that need plenty of maintenance. Do you really need as much as you think? If so, fine, you just need to be sure and be clear about it.

So what's your excuse? What do you want money for? It might be to free you from having a job, or it might not even be for yourself but to support causes you believe in. Set your own agenda, my friend, and keep it to yourself. But I do recommend you write it down, because it makes it so much more real. It is a useful exercise to look back on one day and see if your dream and achievements match.

> WE ALL SPEND ON WHAT
> WE THINK WILL SATISFY US,
> MAKE US HAPPY

RULE 5

Understand that money begets money

There is no greater truth than this – money makes money. It likes clustering together. It breeds quietly and quickly like rabbits. It prefers to hang out in big groups. Money makes money. The rich get richer; the poor get poorer. That's life. Yes, it is sad. But it does seem to be a fact. Now we can work hard ourselves and do something about it or we can sit around moaning and become part of the problem. The choice, as always, is entirely yours.

If you do want to do something about it, then it seems to make sense to me to make a tidy sum and use your money wisely to help the less fortunate than you. Or do whatever with it you so choose.

Once you have some money you'll be astonished at how quickly it can grow. I recommend you understand and learn the concept of compound interest as quickly as possible. And no, I am not going to tell you anything about it except it's vitally important that you know about it and make it a cornerstone in your building of wealth. The reason I'm not going to tell you anything about it is, firstly, this isn't that sort of a book and, secondly, I'm not going to do all the work for you. That would be too easy and you'd learn nothing. My observation is that wealthy people get the idea of compound interest and the rest of us don't.

If you spend all you get, then this Rule will never work for you; it'll never get your money working for you. You have to set aside money for breeding purposes. If you ran a rabbit farm and killed and ate all your rabbits, you wouldn't have any left to keep going. Forget the rabbit farm – you're going to start a money farm. Your money will breed. You can then reinvest some and spend some – but you can't spend it all or you'll have no more rabbits. Look, this stuff is pretty basic but it is amazing how many people simply don't get it. But you do now. You have been given the best tip I can give you.

- Put some money aside for breeding purposes.
- Cream a little off for spending.
- Reinvest the bulk to build up a good and healthy stock.
- Keep it to yourself.

MONEY MAKES MONEY.

THE RICH GET RICHER

It's harder to manage yourself than it is to manage your money

So how well do you know yourself? Pretty well? Not at all? Vaguely? We think we know ourselves until we come to give up smoking, lose weight, get fit, get rich. And then we realise we are lazier, have less willpower, less determination, make less effort, get too easily dissuaded, fall by the wayside too readily.

If I wanted to tuck you under my wing and make you wealthy, the first thing I would need to know is: 'Do you have what it takes to be wealthy? Are you determined enough? Will you work hard enough? Will you stick at it? Do you have backbone? Stamina? Guts? Relentless focus?' You see, if you don't, the chances are you won't succeed. I'm not trying to put you off. I am trying to make you see that making money is a skill that can be taught – as long as the person is ready and willing to learn and apply themselves diligently.

If you decided you wanted to win Wimbledon you would have needed to start playing tennis when you were about five and have been winning junior championships by the time you were fourteen. It's the same with money. You can't expect an overweight, middle-aged person to suddenly be in the final.

When I was a young struggling student I once sold a valuable book so I could eat. I made a direct choice between owning something that was going to increase in value, and thus potentially make me wealthy, and having a slap-up meal for one. You see what I mean? I, in essence, chose – at that time anyway – to be poor rather than wealthy. I saw the same book recently in a bookshop and, believe me, I made a bad call that day.

And what I have noticed is that the wealthy – when they are starting out anyway – have enormous drive and are prepared to make enormous sacrifices. They manage themselves and forgo instant rewards for bigger payback in the longer term. Self-control and delayed gratification are useful arts to learn.

> # THE FIRST THING I WOULD NEED TO KNOW IS: 'DO YOU HAVE WHAT IT TAKES TO BE WEALTHY?'

Only by looking wealthy can you become wealthy

I once watched a man looking at a job vacancy board. He was dressed in scruffy trainers, wore a hood (up), was unshaven and slouched with his hands in his pockets. You just knew he was going to go for job interviews dressed like that – and fail to get them. And then he'd claim it was unfair, nobody would give him a break, life sucks and so on.

I've held many job interviews and have always been seriously under-impressed with the way people turned up. The lack of effort is always staggering – as is the lack of research and interest. 'Why do you want to work for this company?' 'Dunno.' 'What do we do here?' 'Dunno.'

I'm trying not to be an old reactionary here. But I can't fail to notice that the lack of effort is directly related to the lack of results. The poor look poor. Not because they have to. They wear a uniform that marks them out. If they change that uniform they change their circumstances because people will react differently to them. We aren't too far removed from the other great apes and they relate to each other based a lot on how they move and look. Those who look weak and needy are treated as such. The powerful will strut and look confident. What I am suggesting is that you need to look powerful and confident. We should all look powerful and confident.

Ah, but how can we afford to dress as if we are more wealthy? Come on, come on. I expected better of you. Think laterally. Gorillas do it with no clothes at all. It's about the way you walk rather than what you wear. It's about the overall image you project.

But this doesn't mean you can get away with dressing inappropriately or badly – anyone can dress smartly. Borrow a decent outfit or buy a good one cheaply (no, no, don't buy full price and just put it on your credit card). For the interview for my first casino job, I bought a fabulous jacket from a charity shop – double breasted, wide satin lapels – and proper bow tie you had to tie yourself (none of those rubbish ones on elastic for me). I practised for hours until I got it right and turned up for the first night looking more James Bond than trainee. I made a dramatic impression. Obviously I had got it wrong and had to go and buy a simple black suit from the high street afterwards, but I was remembered as somehow standing out, stylish not scruffy. And I got offered the plum trainee job despite not being in any way qualified for it.

This stuff works you know. Dress wealthy and people will assume you are and treat you accordingly. Learn style, class and how the wealthy dress. Look poor and you'll get poor service. And whatever you do, no bling. Yes, rich rap stars can get away with it but you can't. Nor can I. Restrained elegance is what we shall aim for. Old money. Quality. Simple lines. Good haircut. Clean nails. You know the sort of stuff I mean.

YOU NEED TO LOOK POWERFUL AND CONFIDENT

Know yourself – solo, duo or team player

If you are going to change direction – in this case to prosperity from wherever it is you are now – then you need to know:

- your strengths and weaknesses
- what you are good at – and bad at obviously (and this isn't the same as strengths and weaknesses).

For example, I'm good at broad strokes, big picture stuff but I'm not the greatest when it comes to detail.

Get what I'm on about? You just have to know yourself pretty well and then you will be confident in the areas you are good at, can brush up in areas you are weak, can trade on your strengths and get someone else to do all the stuff you are bad at (or haven't yet learned or researched or studied).

And then you've got to know if you are at your best working as part of a partnership, a team or going it alone. Personally I always need the steadying hand of a partner to curb some of my business excesses – an overwhelming tendency to shoot from the hip, be a bit undiplomatic at times, to rush headlong into things, to spend money wastefully on advertising and not to attend to the detail. I am, however, really bad in a team of more than two. So if a business opportunity comes up that requires teamwork I know I can turn it down or tailor it in some way, because I know if I say yes, I will make a pig's ear of it. If, however, it requires a partnership, I'm much more likely to be interested.

I am also good working alone. I make decisions easily (not always the right ones but at least I don't prevaricate), I am happy in my own company for long periods and don't need to bounce ideas off anyone to make them seem real. I can travel well alone and can speak up for myself. See what I mean about knowing yourself?

You have to do this exercise if you are to forge ahead with the rest of the moneymakers. Questions to ask:

- Am I good on my own or do I need other people around me?

- Do I have a role to play in a team and feel happier in that role?

- Can I work well with just one trusted partner?

- Do I know where my strengths and weaknesses are and do I know the difference?

- Do I know what I am good and bad at?

My business partner says we work well together because we are the 'brains and brawn'. The only trouble is we both see ourselves as the brains and the other as the brawn. Oh well.

> # I ALWAYS NEED THE STEADYING HAND OF A PARTNER TO CURB SOME OF MY BUSINESS EXCESSES

Don't try to get rich too quickly

We've already said you need to think long term. Trying to get rich quick only leads to disappointment and over-anxious hustling. And you do need to build a good base or your financial castle can topple at the first gust of wind. The longer you take to make your money, the more diverse you'll be with investments and income streams.

The quicker you make your money, the more likely it'll be a single strand and thus easy to break.

Getting rich over time usually means you'll:

- build long-term income streams
- be insured against recession or sudden and negative market downturns
- have time to have a life as well – that old work/home relationship is less likely to be fractured
- be better at making money honestly and decently
- have time to make the relevant adjustments and thus not so likely to rush out and spend inappropriately
- gain the experience necessary for long-term financial security as you go along.

If you make your money too quickly there is a tendency to:

- spend it inappropriately
- not have time to learn to handle it well
- risk losing it by having your income coming from one area only.

If you really do want to earn a lot quickly you might like to take a leaf out of 79-year-old Stella Liebeck's book. She sued McDonald's because she burnt herself with spilt hot coffee and was awarded initially $2.9 million – later knocked down to a mere $640,000.

This may not have been a deliberate game plan but it did pay off – and quickly. Personally I would rather make my money slowly and enjoyably and not have to sue anyone to get it – or win the lottery, or have a close relative die, or have to marry someone inappropriate merely because they had a quid or two. Make your money slowly and you'll enjoy it more. It will last longer and you'll sleep nights.

> # THE LONGER YOU TAKE TO MAKE YOUR MONEY, THE MORE DIVERSE YOU'LL BE WITH INVESTMENTS AND INCOME STREAMS

Know when to stop

What? I can hear a gasp of surprise. Know when to stop?! Didn't you say earlier that you shouldn't rest on your laurels or they will wilt? Yes I did, but that was when you were starting to get results, not when you'd done really well and were wealthier than you thought you ever would be. Look, there has to come a time when enough is enough. There has to come a time when you want to:

- spend more time with your family

- enjoy your life

- have fun

- go travelling

- get the work/life balance tipped a bit in favour of the life

- use your time to pass on what you have learned to others.

Of course you might be able to do all of these without giving up the gaining wealth ideal. But it is the focus that stops perhaps. Being driven to gain prosperity is a good thing. But once gained, you should return to the fold so to speak. I am always impressed by people like Lady Gaga, who devotes a great deal of her time and money to the charitable causes she believes in.

And Warren Buffet has done the same – pledging to give away 99 percent of his fortune by the end of his lifetime. I know he's playing around with sums well into the billions but his heart is in the right place. He's probably living on the interest on the interest on the interest on the interest . . . These sorts of people are where this rule comes from. In fact the greatest philanthropist of the last 100 years, in terms of the amount of money donated, was Jamsetji Tata – founder of India's Tata group – who donated 102 billion dollars to education and healthcare over his lifetime.

You're thinking that you aren't anywhere in the same league. No, but you can still have an end game strategy whereby you build an 'enough is enough' clause into your plan. Otherwise where do you stop? How much is enough? Where do you draw the line? There is an Arab saying: 'If you have much, give of your wealth; if you have little, give of your heart.' So when you get a lot, give some of it away.

I'm not going to browbeat you about giving to charity but I am suggesting that knowing when you've got enough money is important. I know there is an expression that you can't have too much of a good thing but focusing on prosperity is only one part of a rich and varied life and you can be too dedicated.

> # THERE HAS TO COME
> # A TIME WHEN ENOUGH
> # IS ENOUGH

THE RULES OF
PARENTING

With six children it's easy to see why parenting jumped out at me as an area of life which is full of helpful Rules, if only we know what they are. By this point I'd been watching other parents – and making plenty of mistakes of my own – for well over 30 years. I'd observed patterns of behaviour, helpful and otherwise, for decades. I met parents of my youngest child's friends behaving just the same way as parents I'd encountered when my eldest was a toddler. I'd learnt loads from other parents that I'd had the chance to put into practice myself. I'd tried out lots of Rules I'd observed, and found that things went better when I remembered to use them.

They famously say there's no book that tells you how to be a parent. I wanted to put together a set of principles that would help parents feel a bit less at sea, and a bit more confident that they were doing the right thing. After all, we love our children so much that it matters desperately to us that we get it right (or at least not very wrong). We'll never be perfect – that's one of the Rules we need to embrace – but that doesn't mean we don't want to give it our damnedest.

My youngest child was not yet at school when I put these Rules together, while my oldest had already produced my first grandchild, so I was well aware that parenting doesn't stop when they hit 18. Given that scope, I divided *The Rules of Parenting* into ten sections:

- Rules for staying sane

- Attitude Rules

- Everyday Rules

- Discipline Rules

- Personality Rules

- Sibling Rules

- School Rules

- Teenage Rules

- Crisis Rules

- Grown-up Rules.

I was really keen to learn which Rules got the most votes for this book, and interestingly there was a really wide, broad spread. I'd wondered if there'd be an emphasis on teenage Rules, for example, or sibling Rules. However that wasn't the case. The top voted Rules were 'Relax' and 'Treat your child with respect'. Like so many Rules I've identified over the years, they seem completely obvious, but how many people do we know who don't follow them? Indeed, can we swear that we follow them ourselves without fail, even on a bad day? These two Rules are absolute back to basics Rules (many I've discovered over the years are less intuitive), but clearly readers recognised just how easy it is to forget the basics in the hurly-burly of trying to raise a family.

Relax

So who are the best parents you know? The ones who have a seemingly instinctive ability to say and do the things that will result in happy, confident, well-balanced children? Have you ever wondered what makes them so good at it? Now think about the ones you privately don't think are much cop. Why not?

All the best parents I know have one key thing in common. They're relaxed about it. And all the worst ones are hung up on something. Maybe they're not stressed out about how good they are as parents (perhaps they should be) but they're hung up about something that affects their ability to be a really good parent.

I know a couple of parents who are neurotically clean and tidy. Their children have to take their shoes off at the door or the whole world falls apart. Even if the shoes are clean. They get really uptight if their children leave anything out of place or make any kind of a mess (even if it gets cleared up later). It makes it impossible for the kids just to relax and enjoy themselves, in case they get grass stains on their trousers, or knock over the ketchup bottle.

I have another friend who is so obsessively competitive that his children are under huge pressure to win every friendly game they ever play. And one who frets excessively every time her child grazes his knees. I bet you can think of plenty of similar examples among people you know.

The really good parents I've encountered, on the other hand, expect their children to be noisy, messy, bouncy, squabbly, whingy and covered in mud. They take it all in their stride. They know they've got 18 years to turn these small creatures into respectable grown-ups, and they pace themselves. No rush to get them acting like adults – they'll get there in good time.

Between you and me, this Rule gets easier with time, though some people still never master it the way true Rules parents do. It's much harder to relax fully with your first baby than with your last teenager to leave home. With babies, you need to focus on the essentials – a healthy baby that isn't too hungry or too uncomfortable – and don't sweat the rest of it. It doesn't matter if their poppers are done up wrong, or you didn't find time to bath them today, or you've gone away for the weekend without anything for them to sleep in (yes, I have a friend who has done this, and no, she didn't sweat it, being a Rules parent).

Much better altogether if you can get to the end of each day, put your feet up with a glass of wine or a G&T,[9] and say cheerfully to each other, 'What the hell ... they're all still alive so we must have got something right'.

> REALLY GOOD PARENTS EXPECT
> THEIR CHILDREN TO BE NOISY,
> MESSY, BOUNCY, SQUABBLY,
> WHINGY AND COVERED IN MUD

---

[9] No, I'm not encouraging parents to use alcohol to get them through. Just relax!

Look pleased to see them

Now here's something that really gets my goat. I can't count the number of parents I've seen do this. Their child comes in from school or an afternoon out, and as they walk through the door they're greeted with, 'Take those muddy shoes off!' Or, 'Homework, now! Before you do anything else'.

I have a friend who once came home from school in the middle of the day with a huge bump on her head, after a fall in the gym. This was in the days when you were allowed to go home on your own after something like that happened. Her mum was busy mopping the kitchen floor as my friend appeared in the doorway. The mum looked up with wrinkled brow and said, 'You can't come in. The floor's wet'.

How are these children supposed to know their parents love them? After all, their mum and dad greet the dog, the grandparents, their children's friends, even the postman[10] more warmly than that.

The alternative practised by some parents is just to ignore the children when they come in, as if they were part of the furniture. This is just as bad, since giving them no attention at all is arguably as bad as giving them negative attention (that's wibble-speak for shouting at them).

Everyone is generally rushed at breakfast time on school days. But it takes no time at all to be friendly, and frankly anything that makes the kids a little bit less grumpy while you're trying to

---

[10] No offence to postmen. In fact we have two postmen and they can be relied on to give me a friendly greeting to start the day. They're known as Worm (he always turns up early) and Grub, though not to their faces.

get their hair brushed or shovel some food down them has to be worthwhile, doesn't it?

How hard can it be to give them a smile, and maybe a hug (if they haven't reached the age where they won't let you)? It's only a small thing, but it makes a huge difference to your kids. They just want to know that you're happy to see them.

And if their shoes really are filthy and you've just cleaned the kitchen floor (one might ask why, when the kids were about to appear in muddy shoes), you can still use humour to stop them in their tracks and then give them hugs and kisses for co-operating.

HOW HARD CAN IT BE TO GIVE THEM A SMILE, AND MAYBE A HUG?

RULE 3

Treat your child with respect

I know a mother who is always issuing her children with instructions: 'Eat your lunch.' 'Get in the car.' 'Clean your teeth.' The other day I heard her complaining about how hard it is to get her children to say please and thank you. Now you and I know exactly what her problem is, but she can't see it.

It's frighteningly easy to do, though. Children are supposed to do what you say, whereas other adults don't have to. So you ask the grown-ups nicely, but you just tell the kids what to do. The problem is that the kids don't see it like that. They don't notice how you speak to everyone else (after all, kids never listen). They just speak to you in the way you speak to them.

If your children have any sense they'll take more notice of what you do than of anything you say. So not only can you not blame them for skimping on the niceties if you do, but actually they should be congratulated on following your example.

Your children deserve respect, of course, simply because they're human. But on top of that, you won't get respect back from them if you don't show it. You won't be undermining your authority. Your kids will soon learn that 'Clean your teeth please' or 'Would you lay the table?' might sound like a request but actually they don't have a choice. You'll just be teaching them manners in the best way possible – by demonstration.

It's not only manners that they need to learn by example. You should never break promises to them, never lie to them (Father Christmas doesn't count), and never swear in front of them if you don't want them to copy you. If you do these things, you are telling your kids loud and clear (if not in so many words) that they are less important than other people and they don't matter.

Now we know that isn't true. It's important that your children know it too.

If you love your children more than anyone else (except your partner), then they deserve your respect more than anyone else, not less. That way, they'll learn to treat other people with respect too. There, that's the problem of 'What's the younger generation coming to?' sorted.

> YOUR CHILDREN DESERVE
> RESPECT, OF COURSE, SIMPLY
> BECAUSE THEY'RE HUMAN

RULE 4

Use praise wisely

Well done! You've made it to Rule 4[11]. You're nearly half way to being a fully paid-up Rules parent.

I hope that made you feel encouraged – that's the purpose of praise. And we Rules parents know that if we're doing our job properly, our praise will be one of the biggest motivators for our kids. You wouldn't let their birthday go by without giving them a present, so don't let good achievements go by without giving them praise.

Ah, but it's not quite that simple, is it? How many parents do you know who don't use praise as wisely as they might? You have to give them the right amount, in the right way.

The expression, 'You can't have too much of a good thing' certainly doesn't apply to praise. That doesn't mean you should be stingy, but you should give praise in proportion to your child's achievements. If you over-praise them you devalue the currency. If you tell them they're superbly brilliant when they do something pretty average, what will you say when they do something really brilliant? And if every little thing they achieve is rewarded with copious praise, they'll be terrified of failing you. And they don't need that kind of pressure.

A lot of parents forget to praise their child for behaving well, because they take it for granted. But children really want to hear that you noticed how good they were: 'Well done for not picking your nose in front of Auntie Myrtle,' or 'You must be exhausted, but you're still managing not to moan. That's really good.' This is what persuades them that it's worth being good next time.

You can recognise your child's achievements with thanks as well as praise. That takes off some of the pressure, and allows you to

---

[11] Rule 28 in *The Rules of Parenting*

acknowledge them without being effusive. What's more, it's a great way of reinforcing good behaviour, and reassuring them that you notice when they get things right, not just when they go wrong. 'Thanks for hanging up the towel after your bath.' 'Thanks for doing your homework without needing to be reminded.' 'It was good to come home to a tidy kitchen – thank you.'

Now, one last point about praise before you've mastered this Rule. Which of the following do you think your child would most like to hear: 'What a lovely drawing!' or 'What a lovely drawing – I do like the way you've managed to make the horse look as if it's really moving. How did you do that?' Yep – be specific with your praise if you can, and ask them questions too. That will really make them glow.

> # YOU HAVE TO GIVE THEM THE RIGHT AMOUNT, IN THE RIGHT WAY

Make sure they know what's important

Hang on – I haven't quite done with praise yet. OK, now we know how to give them praise effectively. But have you ever stopped to think about what you praise your child for? Think about it now.

I know parents who praise their children most frequently for winning things. In some cases it's sports, in others it's school work. I know others whose praise is largely focused on polite behaviour. Or looking beautifully turned out. Or being 'good'.

The things we choose to praise our children for tell them more about our values than almost anything else. This is how our children assess what really matters in life. If they get all the best responses from you for looking beautiful, or for winning, or for eating everything on their plate, this is what they will unconsciously assume is the most important thing. They'll put all their efforts into it in order to gain your approval, and will start out in life putting huge emphasis on these things.

This means you have a huge responsibility to praise them for the right things. If you always praise them for doing well at school but never for behaving well, what does that tell them about your values? Are you more likely to praise them for winning than for trying hard? No, of course you're not, you're a Rules parent. But a lot of other parents would.

That doesn't mean you can't ever say 'Well done' if they're pleased with themselves for coming top of the class, or winning their race. But be conscious of the balance you give them.

On the plus side, praise is a hugely effective way to imbue your children with the values that matter to you. Telling them, 'I was impressed by the way you took the trouble to include Ali in your group when she was feeling new and shy' impresses on your child that kindness and considerateness are important qualities. Likewise, 'I admire the way you enrolled on that climbing course even though you were nervous', or 'It doesn't matter that you didn't come top – what I noticed was that you put in such a big effort'.

As a parent, it helps to be aware of the values that matter most to you, and to look out for opportunities to acknowledge those things in your child. It's a positive way to use praise (while still keeping it in proportion) to encourage your child to be hard working, thoughtful, unselfish, courageous, determined and kind. And whatever else you think matters.

> ## ARE YOU MORE LIKELY TO PRAISE THEM FOR WINNING THAN FOR TRYING HARD? NO, OF COURSE YOU'RE NOT, YOU'RE A RULES PARENT

RULE 6

Schooling isn't the same as education

I've known people leave school at 16 or 18 and know nothing – except perhaps their times tables and where Burkina Faso is and what the repeal of the corn laws was all about (beats me). In other words, information. That's what school gives you: information. OK, and a few analytical skills such as long division and grammar, many of which you may never use again. Some of it is useful, such as foreign languages, but much of it apparently has no value at all.

Don't get me wrong, I'm not knocking school. It teaches you how to learn – which is a useful skill for the rest of your life – but it takes 10 or 12 years or more to do it. And think about all the things it *doesn't* teach your kids during those formative years. How to think for themselves, how to change a light bulb, how to be assertive, how to stay out of debt, how to tell when a fight's brewing, how to resolve arguments amicably, how to treat people with respect, what to do when the car breaks down, how to face your fears, how to be a good loser, how to be a good winner . . .

'But school does teach you how to win and lose', I hear you say. 'What's sports day all about?' Yes, I know school gives you lots of practice at some of these things (and none at others), but they don't teach you how to do it well. They let you keep losing badly every time if you're so inclined. In any case, the things your kids get lots of practice at in school are all things they could practise just as well outside school. Because it's being in a group of kids that teaches them what behaviour is and isn't socially acceptable. The teachers have nothing to do with it. They can learn that just as well in any group of kids – in a local youth group, or football club, or down at the rec.

The point of all this is that schooling your child is not at all the same thing as educating them. Schooling is important, but not half so important as a good education. It's the school's job to school them (the clue's in the name) but it's your job to educate them. Don't expect the school to do it for you.

I know kids who have been home-educated and ended up much more capable, rounded and mature people than children who've been through full-time schooling. Which rather demonstrates that school isn't necessary for a good education. I'm not telling you to home-educate your child (unless you want to). I'm just saying you shouldn't rely on the school to give your child anything useful except information, and the odd practical skill such as how to play the recorder or dissect a frog. The rest is down to you.

> # THAT'S WHAT SCHOOL GIVES YOU: INFORMATION

Remember Newton's Third Law

The thing is, you love your kids desperately. So it's incredibly hard to watch your teenager making mistakes that you think will come back to bite them later on. Over the years you've got used to letting them make small mistakes – helping themselves to too much pudding, or riding their bike too fast downhill. As time goes on, the mistakes get bigger.

So now you have to watch them drink too much at their mate's party, or wear clothes that are far too low-cut (or high-cut). Maybe you even have to stand back when they decide to leave school at 16, when you'd hoped they'd go to university, or jack in a brilliant Saturday job because it's too much effort getting up in the morning. It's a much bigger deal than letting your two-year-old take too much pudding. The stakes are getting higher.

And worst of all, you may even have to watch them repeating your mistakes. Dropping science just because they hate the teacher when they could have a brilliant career ahead of them. Or saving all their money for a gap year when the time comes, and then blowing it in a moment of madness on a car that doesn't even go properly. You could have told them. You probably did tell them. Quite possibly loudly and forcibly . . . But then, did you listen to your parents when *they* told you all those years ago?

Unless your child is putting themselves in serious danger, you really do have to put up with it. Sometimes even if it's dangerous you have no choice. The more you try to tell them, the more you push them in the opposite direction. They're looking for something to kick at, to rebel against, because they're programmed to. The more force you use, the more they'll use. Remember Newton's Third Law of Motion? For every action there is an equal and opposite reaction. He could equally well have called it the First Law of Teenagers.

So what can you do when you see them going wrong? You can tell them what you think, but don't tell them what to do. And tell them in the way you'd tell a grown-up and an equal. Not, 'I'll tell you what I think! I think you're a fool!' More along the lines of, 'It's your decision, but have you thought how you'll fund your gap year if you spend your money on this?' Talk to them like an adult and maybe they'll respond like an adult. And if not this time, maybe next time. They'll certainly be quicker to ask your advice if they know it will be given as an equal.

> ## DID YOU LISTEN TO YOUR PARENTS ALL THOSE YEARS AGO?

Don't look under the mattress

Teenagers get up to things you don't want to know about. Of course, you do know about them really, which is why you're worried. If you were entirely ignorant you'd be much happier.

Look, take it from me, your daughter has gone further than you'd like with her partner. Your son has watched porn. They've both tried at least a drag of a cigarette by now. And they've almost certainly been offered drugs but they won't have any evidence of it hanging around in their room so there's no point looking. Happy? Good. Now you don't need to look under the mattress or read their secret diary.

You're not going to find anything that thousands of parents before you haven't found. In fact, you're probably not going to find anything that your own parents didn't find. And what are you going to do about it – confront your teenagers? I think not. You'll severely damage your relationship and they'll just keep the stuff under the floorboards instead.

Maybe you should think back to the things you got up to as a teenager that you didn't want your parents to know about. Maybe you even get up to things nowadays that you'd rather not tell your parents. See? Your kids are just being perfectly normal teenagers. And if you don't make a big deal out of all those perfectly normal teenagery things they're getting up to, they're much more likely to come and tell you if anything gets out of hand or is a real problem for them. And that's the really important point. If you act like all that stuff under the mattress is normal, they'll feel they can talk to you without fear of an irrational response.

There's simply no point worrying yourself. By this stage you have to rely on what you've taught them over the last dozen years or so.

And follow Rule 7 – the more of a hard time you give them, the worse they'll get. So don't give them a hard time.

And, on the plus side, the very fact that you don't look under their mattress or read their diary will strengthen your relationship with them. They'll respect you for preserving their privacy (obviously they won't say this), and for having a realistic and modern enough outlook to let them get on with being teenagers undisturbed.

> **TEENAGERS GET UP TO THINGS YOU DON'T WANT TO KNOW ABOUT. OF COURSE, YOU DO KNOW ABOUT THEM REALLY, WHICH IS WHY YOU'RE WORRIED**

You can't fix everything

Oh, this is a toughie. What we parents want most of all is to make everything alright for our kids. If they hurt themselves, we kiss them better. If they're in trouble, we help them sort it out. If they're sad, we hug them. If someone is mean to them, we intervene.

But sometimes our kids have to face really big things that we can't sort out for them. And the feeling of being impotent to help them is a terrible one. There are few things in life worse than watching your child suffer and being unable to take away their pain. But it can happen. When someone dies, you can't bring them back however much your child misses and loves them. Sometimes your child is ill in a way you can't fix. Or their other parent leaves and just isn't there for them when they should be.

It's an important lesson for a kid to learn: stuff happens and some-times there's nothing anybody can do. It's a tough lesson to learn the hard way when they're so young. And watching them learn it can be heartbreaking. But learn it they must, sooner or later, and you have no control over when life decides to teach it to them. All you can do is comfort them through it, but you can't stop it hurting.

So this Rule is about accepting that there's nothing you can do. It doesn't have to be your fault, and no one else could do any better than you. It's just a bummer, end of story. Don't beat yourself up, because you don't deserve it. Things are hard enough for you already. You're probably going through the same pain yourself, as well as watching your child suffer, and you really don't need to dump anything more on yourself. Just give yourself a hug and a bit of sympathy.[12]

---

[12] And maybe chocolate.

And remember, your child isn't expecting you to work miracles. They're not daft and they know there's nothing you can do. All you can do for them right now is give them your love and lots of big hugs, so just do that. It will probably help both of you to feel a little bit better.

IT'S JUST A BUMMER, END OF STORY

Don't guilt-trip them

This is a big lever some parents use to control their grown-up children: guilt. Some of them lay it on really thick too, but our children are sensitive creatures and even the most subtle guilt-tripping makes its point.

The most common subject of these guilt trips is the amount of attention the 'child' pays to their parent. Comments like, 'Your sister phones every week' or 'I know you're ever so busy at weekends. I wish I could say the same', are all intended to make the kids feel bad about not spending more time with their parents. Even, 'Oh, it'll be so lonely here once you leave home'.

Look, let's get something straight. Your kids owe you nothing. *Nothing*. I don't care how much blood, sweat and tears went into those first 18 years of their lives. They didn't ask to be born, and having chosen to have kids, you became responsible for all that effort. You owe them loads, but they owe you zilch. So it's never OK to give your kids the impression that they owe you anything – time, attention, money or anything else.

Of course, if you're a good Rules parent your children will want to do loads for you. And the fact that they don't actually owe it to you should make it all the more precious when they choose to give it to you. Good kids will look after you in your old age because you've earned it and they love you. Some kids look after their parents out of guilt, but they don't enjoy it and they resent their parents for it, and that's not what you want. You want time and attention that your kids give you freely because you deserve it. And you'll never get that if you guilt-trip them.

You must have friends who say things like, 'I've got to go and see my father this weekend. I haven't seen him for a month', or 'I'm busy this evening – my mum calls every Wednesday and it always takes me at least two hours to get her off the phone'. Maybe you've even said such things yourself. But you don't want your kids talking about you like that. You want them to say, 'I can't make it – I really want to see my parents this weekend' or 'I haven't spoken to Mum properly for a couple of weeks and I do miss a good chat with her'. So lay off the guilt because however much they'll do for you through guilt, they'll do twice as much without the guilt, and you'll know they're enjoying it.

In fact, the best gift of all you can give your children is independence. Not theirs; yours. If you are emotionally, socially and financially independent, you free them of all guilt. That way, anything they do for you they'll be doing out of love.

> ## YOUR KIDS OWE YOU
> ## NOTHING. *NOTHING*

THE RULES OF LOVE

It was only ever a matter of time before I put together the countless Rules I'd observed over the years when it came to love. I'd been through an unpleasant divorce (what other kind is there?) and was lucky enough to follow it with a second, very successful marriage. I brought to that second marriage many Rules I'd learnt first time round, along with many more I'd observed other people follow.[13]

However, my wife is far from the only person I love. There's my children, my wider family, my friends ... The bulk of the book needed to be about romantic love but I wanted to do justice to those other aspects of love too. When we first fall in love it can feel as if we're in a bubble, but before long normal life reasserts itself, and other relationships are essential to our happiness too.

If you can build a really strong and loving partnership with one person, and keep it like that for life, you have the best possible foundation for success in every other part of your life. And when things do go wrong elsewhere, you couldn't ask for a better support to cope with them. It's not easy though, is it? It can seem like a minefield but, as with everything else, if you understand the guiding principles – the Rules – and learn to follow them, you'll have the best possible chance.

When you watch people trying to negotiate this trickiest but vital part of their lives, you start to realise that the Rules that apply to finding that elusive right person are very different from the Rules for staying with them happily.

---

[13] To be fair to my wife, she made the odd contribution too.

Every good relationship has two phases. In the first stage you meet, fall in love, and decide you want to be together. That can take anything from a few weeks to a few years. The second phase can last the rest of your lives, and calls on a whole new set of Rules to keep the relationship strong and loving for both of you.

I took that into account when I organised *The Rules of Love*, so there are five sections:

- Rules for finding love

- Relationship Rules

- Family Rules

- Friendship Rules

- Rules for everyone.

You might be interested to know that the top-voted Rule in this book, 'Choose someone who makes you laugh' was in fact the most nominated Rule across all ten books. As it's probably my own personal top Rule of love, it was very encouraging to see how many other people feel the same way.

Choose someone who makes you laugh

I've put this Rule first, because it's the absolutely most important thing of all in a relationship. If you choose your partner for their looks, their status, even the rest of their personality, you could regret it eventually. Anyway, lots of those things can get lost along the way. Even personality traits can change – a confident person can be shattered by an emotional trauma, a patient person can become irritable and frustrated through illness or pain.

But a sense of humour will last you long after everything else has gone. When you're both sitting there in your rocking chairs, decades after retirement, and the kids have long since grown up, it may be all you have left. And if it is, it will be enough.

Laughter is worth its weight in gold. A sense of humour is a very personal thing, and some people just make us laugh more than others. When you find the person who really makes you laugh more than anyone else, marry them. That's my advice. Assuming they are the right sex for you. You're almost guaranteed to fancy them, because anyone who makes you laugh will be hugely attractive, even if they're not physically what you'd been anticipating.

OK, I'm being a little extreme here, but only slightly. Personally I married the person who made me laugh more than anyone else, and it was absolutely the right thing to do. But maybe you'll prefer to go for the second or third funniest person you meet. Just don't compromise on the sense of humour, because it really is the top priority.

I'll tell you another thing to look for. You don't just want someone who makes you laugh generally, although that's essential. The best thing of all is to find someone who can make you laugh at yourself. That will get you through life more smoothly than anything else.

I have a friend whose wife died a few years ago, and he says that one of the things he misses most is being able to laugh at himself. He hadn't realised how much she helped him to do that, or how essential it was to his happiness. He says he takes himself far too seriously these days and gets stressed about things that she would have got him chuckling about.

So the next time you meet someone with gorgeous legs, or sexy eyes, or a cute smile, don't be seduced straight away. See if they can tickle you without touching first.

> **A SENSE OF HUMOUR WILL LAST YOU LONG AFTER EVERYTHING ELSE HAS GONE**

You can't change people

Suppose you're naturally tidy. I mean really neurotically tidy. Can't stand to leave the washing up for later and always put away everything immediately after use. And imagine you ended up with a partner who liked to spread their possessions about and actually only felt comfortable with clutter. Would you become a messy person to keep them happy? Then why would you expect them to become tidy?

If you're not actually tidy you might be wondering what the problem would be, but if you're one of nature's tidy people you'll probably be thinking that would be a struggle, and an unreasonable request. And you'd be right.

The fact is that you can't ask people to change, and even if they wanted to they couldn't do it. Sure, they can modify their behaviour, but they can't change their personality. You might persuade your messy partner to hang up the bathroom towel instead of leaving it on the floor, but I bet they'll hang it up all crooked and it will still drive you mad. That's because you can't turn them into a tidy person – only a messy one who hangs up the towel. Meantime the kitchen will be a tip, and the floor of the car will be disgusting (in your view, but not theirs).

And it's not just a question of being messy or tidy. You can't stop someone being irresponsible, or football-obsessed, or a workaholic, or shy, or easily stressed.

So if you can't live with these characteristics, don't get involved. Whatever you do, don't embark on a relationship with someone thinking, 'I can't cope with this bit of their personality, but that's OK – I'll change it'. You won't, you know. You'll just make both of you miserable.

I know no one is exactly perfect – everyone can be irritating from time to time in a relationship (including you) – but you're looking for someone whose irritating habits are worth putting up with, not for someone who you can mould to your personal requirements.

And be warned that this also applies to the big stuff that could make you very unhappy. If you meet someone who is perfect apart from being emotionally withdrawn, or physically abusive, or serially unfaithful, you won't change that either. Please don't kid yourself. They might keep the behaviour in check for the first few months or years, but sooner or later, when the euphoria wears off and the stress of normal life returns, they will go back to their old ways. Don't say I didn't warn you.

> # EVERYONE CAN BE IRRITATING FROM TIME TO TIME IN A RELATIONSHIP (INCLUDING YOU)

You can't make someone love you

It's possible this is one of the hardest things to accept when it comes to matters of the heart. You find the person you've been looking for all your life. Trouble is, they don't seem to have realised it.

Maybe you met recently and you're head over heels, but they don't seem very keen. You're hanging on desperately, sure that they must soon realise you are made for each other ... Or maybe you've actually been together as a couple for years – they are very fond of you, after all, and being with you is easy – but deep down you know they don't really love you.

Sooner or, maybe, later they'll tell you that things just aren't working out, but you don't want to hear it. You try to persuade them to give you another chance. Maybe you try to change, to become the person they really want. It's all a bit humiliating really, but you don't see it like that. You think it's worth it to win their love.

Funny thing is, though – it never works. Love just isn't like that. You can jump through any hoops you like, beat yourself up for not being able to match up to their standard (as you see it), damage your confidence and your self-esteem in the process, and still they won't love you. They can't. Maybe they're gentle and apologetic about it, or maybe they're unkind or even brutal.

The same scenario is played out in relationships the world over – where only one of the two is actually in love. Think through some of the couples you know and I bet you can think of examples where this is true.

I know people who have been through this, and have taken months or years to realise there's no hope. Since then, they've found romance with someone who reciprocates their love. And the interesting thing is that everyone I know who has been through this says the same thing: thank goodness that other relationship finally ended, because this is so much better.

You see, however wonderful the object of your affections is, if they don't love you back the relationship will never be that good. Even supposing they *could* love you, if it requires you to keep jumping through all those hoops to hang on to them, it's just not worth it. You need and deserve someone who loves you for who you are, not for who you're pretending or trying to be. So as soon as you realise you're with someone who doesn't love you, you need to be really brave and end the relationship before they do. You'll feel bad about losing them, but great for holding on to your pride, and one day you'll look back and realise how courageous and right a decision it was.

> **MAYBE YOU TRY TO CHANGE, TO BECOME THE PERSON THEY REALLY WANT**

Be nice

You've had a long and tiring day. In fact it's been a difficult week. You get home grumpy and irritable and you need someone to take it out on. Who's there to oblige? Your partner of course. Always available and it's not surprising you're feeling snappy, so what do they expect?

What they might expect is that you'd treat them nicely. If it was a friend standing there as you walked through the door, you'd manage to find it in you to be polite to them, so why not your partner? After all, they should be the most important person in the world to you, so why don't they get the best treatment?

It's so easy to use your partner as a handy sponge to absorb all your angst and to vent your spleen on. But that doesn't make it right. I've known plenty of couples who are snappy and irritable with each other regularly, or even downright rude, simply because they can't be bothered to be nice. Not because either has done anything wrong. None of them have really happy and enviable relationships, mind you.

What's wrong with a bit of old-fashioned civility? What became of 'please' and 'thank you' and 'would you mind'? If you want to feel really positive about what you have together, you need to start by being courteous and respectful to each other. Remember your basic manners, and speak with respect and kindness to one another. Fix them their favourite drink, or give them a little gift for no reason except the best one of all – because you love them. Pay them compliments, help them with mundane tasks even if it's not 'your job' to put up shelves or do the ironing or fetch the shopping in from the car.

If your partner comes home after a tiring day, don't give them a chance to take out their irritation on you. Make them a drink, ask them how they are and listen to what they say. Be interested. Perhaps find some little task you can relieve them of: 'Tell you what, you put your feet up and I'll sort out dinner/walk the dog/get the kids to do their homework.' Run them a hot bath (and maybe add some relaxing oils or light a few candles) and generally make them feel that someone cares. Because you do care.

If you have children, what better example could you set them? In any case, think about the example you're setting your partner. You're asking to be treated in the way you treat them, so you'd better make it good. But that's not why you're doing it. You're not being nice in order to make them be nice back. You're being nice because you love them and that's what they deserve.

WHAT'S WRONG WITH A BIT OF OLD-FASHIONED CIVILITY?

Allow your partner the space to be themselves

After a few months or years together, couples can settle down into a 'couple personality' which is greater than the sum of its parts. You do things together, you socialise together, you find shared interests to follow together.

This is all very lovey-dovey and sweet, but it ignores the fact that you are also separate people. It doesn't matter how much you had in common when you met, your partner has some interests separate from yours. Maybe you met through a passionate hobby and you both want to devote most of your free time to yachting or dog walking or stamp collecting. But even so, you may want to concentrate on different aspects of it,[14] or there may be other lesser interests too.

Your partner needs some time to do their own thing in their own way and even on their own. Maybe they want to meet up with their best mates without you there, or shut themselves away for an hour or so at a time reading poetry or sewing or fixing outboard motors, or become a world expert in pre-1930s Balinese stamps.[15] And you need to give them the time and the space to do that without getting stroppy or jealous or niggly about it.

If you're never out of each other's company, and you both turn into some kind of hybrid creature incorporating bits of both of you, you'll end up losing sight of the person you first fell in love with. That's not going to help your relationship because if that happens, that's when the whole thing loses its sparkle, its magic, and becomes tedious.

---

[14] Please don't ask for details on the different aspects of stamp collecting.

[15] Whatever.

I'm not trying to dictate how much time you spend in each other's company. In fact I'm not trying to dictate anything – I'm just telling you what works if you want to be happy in love. Some couples are rarely apart and yet still manage to respect each other's space. Some rarely socialise without each other. But for most couples, a bit more space helps things along and means that you have something to talk about.

The odds are that you need a bit of space from your partner from time to time. Maybe you need a lot. That's OK (within reason). The important thing is to recognise that when they want to do something on their own, it's not a rejection of you, it's simply an affirmation of who they are. It's their way of touching base and staying happy and if you don't let them do it, you'll lose the person you love.

So no niggling, no irritation, no jealousy, no childish behaviour when your partner tells you they need a bit of space. Be pleased for them and for yourself, because this is what's going to keep your relationship fresh.

> YOU NEED TO GIVE THEM
> THE TIME AND THE SPACE
> WITHOUT GETTING STROPPY
> OR JEALOUS OR NIGGLY

Be the first to say sorry

Grown-ups don't have rows. Sure, they argue, they disagree, they debate. They express their feelings and say when they're hurt or angry or upset. But they don't have the kinds of rows that require an apology to get over them.

Oh, alright then, we do. But that doesn't make it right. From time to time we forget to do the 'When you say ... I feel ...' thing we all know we should, and we behave childishly instead. Don't worry, we all do it. I expect they started it anyway.

The big question is, having fallen out with the person we love, which isn't what we wanted to do of course, what are we going to do about it? And the answer – as you may have guessed from the title of this Rule – is to say sorry. And to say it even before they do.

How do you feel about saying sorry? Can't see why you should? Or do you feel you've lost face, been humiliated, had to swallow your pride? Well, don't. You're a Rules Player and you're big and strong and confident and self-assured enough to do it. I'm not asking you to say sorry publicly in front of 500 people after all. This is just a private apology to your very nearest and dearest. You can manage that.

And what are you apologising for? Isn't it hypocritical to say sorry when you truly feel you were in the right? No, it isn't because that's not what you're saying sorry for. You're saying sorry for allowing a perfectly valid discussion about a difference of views to degenerate to this point. It takes two to argue and you're apologising for being so childish as to let it happen, and for all the mistakes you must have made to reach this point.

Someone has to be the first to acknowledge that childishness has gone on, and as you're a Rules Player it will have to be you. If your partner is a Rules Player too, you'll have to get a move on if you're going to beat them to it. You have to prove that at least one of you can be magnanimous, generous, open, conciliatory and grown up. And with luck they'll respond by showing you that they can be all those things too. They just needed you to remind them.

Whatever it was you fell out over – which may or may not still need resolving once everyone has calmed down – making up and being friends again has got to be better than sulking or stropping was. You both got yourselves into this pickle and it will take both of you to get yourselves out.

Remember, you're apologising for allowing things to get over-heated and out of hand. You're not apologising for your original opinion or action. Unless, of course, you were actually out of order there as well. In which case you will indeed apologise for that too.

> YOU'RE APOLOGISING FOR BEING SO CHILDISH AS TO LET IT HAPPEN, AND FOR ALL THE MISTAKES YOU MUST HAVE MADE TO REACH THIS POINT

Your partner is more important than your kids

Here's a Rule that lots of people come a cropper with. Quite understandably but that's not the point. These Rules are here for your benefit, and just because you have a good excuse for ignoring them doesn't mean you won't still suffer for it. And this is one Rule you really can't ignore.

When your children are little it's easy to put them before your partner, especially if you're the one who spends the most time with them. As they grow older they're still demanding, goodness knows, and what's more it's become habit now to put them first. And then eventually – eventually – they leave home. And what are you left with? A partner who hasn't been the focus of your life for 20-odd years and who you find you've drifted apart from. Which is a shame, because you're now alone with them for the next few decades in all probability. It's that or divorce, and neither will be much fun.

Now I'm not saying that children don't take up a lot of your time. Most of it when they're small. I've had six of them so I do know. And this Rule isn't about your partner getting more time than the kids because that often just isn't possible. But it's crucial that your partner is the primary focus of your life, even while your responsibility and time commitment to the children is greater. I'm not saying you should love them best because there's enough love for everyone and it's a very different kind of love. But never lose sight of the fact that having children at home is temporary (albeit long-term temporary), whereas your partner is for life.

You may not like this Rule but I don't care. This book is not about what should or shouldn't be, it's about what is. And the people who have the strongest and best relationships – which last long and happily after the children have left home – are the ones who follow this Rule.

What's more, your children need you to put your partner first. For one thing, how are they going to find the confidence and energy to leave home if they know they'll be tearing your life apart in the process? This is often a problem for youngest children when their parents have grown apart over the years and they know they are the most important person in at least one of their parents' lives. They feel trapped if they stay and guilty if they go. Some parents even say, 'How will I manage without you?' – but of course you won't because you're a Rules Player.

And of course your kids want to go out into the world and find someone to fall in love with who is more important to them than you are. Just as your partner is – or at least once was – more important to you than your parents. That's going to be pretty difficult for them if it's one-sided. No, for them to be free to find someone else, you have to have someone else too. And that some-one is your partner.

> # THIS ISN'T ABOUT YOUR PARTNER GETTING MORE TIME THAN THE KIDS BECAUSE THAT OFTEN JUST ISN'T POSSIBLE

RULE 8

Contentment is a high aim

You know that feeling you get when you first fall in love? Weak at the knees, stomach churning, can't think about anything else? It's great, isn't it? On the other hand, it puts you on an emotional knife-edge that makes almost everything else, from work to eating, really quite difficult.

Some people get addicted to it. They just don't feel alive unless they're 'in love'. But of course relationships don't stay like that. Sooner or later you become confident and sure enough of your partner not to worry or fret, and you get used to having them around so you don't jump at the sound of the phone. So if you're addicted to falling 'in love', you'll have to keep ditching your partners and finding new people to fall for.

You may be wondering why I keep putting inverted commas round 'in love'. Well, there are two reasons. The first is that you don't have to be in love to have this feeling, and you may be misled. It might actually be lust or infatuation and not love at all. And the other reason is that I don't want to imply that if you don't have this feeling you aren't in love with your partner.

There are very good reasons why this heightened emotional state doesn't last forever. You couldn't function, and the state has a lot to do with nerves and excitement and after a while your relationship will inevitably stop making you nervous, and cease to be as exciting as it was. You can still do exciting things together, but the relationship itself will become reliable, hopefully in the very best of ways.

So what do you end up with if you stick out the relationship past the point where you can't sleep at night and can't think about anything else? Well, that varies of course. For some people what's left isn't really worth having. But for those people who have a combination of luck, good judgement and a grasp of the Rules, what you can end up with if all goes really well is contentment.

Contentment isn't about fireworks, weak knees and flutteriness. Which is why some people completely fail to realise that despite its more subtle charm, contentment is worth a whole lot more than short-term passion. And being content with someone doesn't mean you're no longer 'in love'. It means you are truly and deeply in love in the best sense without any inverted commas.

So don't get hooked on getting that fix of first 'love'. Concentrate on making sure that you follow the Rules so that as the first flush slowly dies down, it is replaced by something that is more reward-ing, companionable, warm, fulfilling and loving. And when that happens, don't think about what you have lost, but about what you've gained. That's contentment – and you should be more than happy with it.

> # CONTENTMENT ISN'T ABOUT FIREWORKS, WEAK KNEES AND FLUTTERINESS

Never be too busy for loved ones

I'm as guilty here as anyone. It's so easy to think, 'I'm tired. I'll give them a call tomorrow', and before you know it a dozen tomorrows have gone by and you still haven't called.

And it's really not good enough. If you want a strong relationship with your family you have to work at it, just as you do with your partner. And that means investing time in it. You need to find time to see them even if they live a long way away, and you need to put effort into calling them between times to keep in touch (note to self). It's so easy to fall into benign neglect. You didn't mean to not speak for three months, it just sort of happened. Well, don't let it.

Of course, your family may not be any better than you at finding time. They may even be worse. But that doesn't let you off the hook: two wrongs don't make a right. If they're useless at it, all the more reason why you need to make the effort. Otherwise you'll find eventually that you don't have a family worthy of the name any more. And that would be really sad.

So forgive your sister for being hopeless at getting round to calling, and your father for being forgetful, and make the call or the journey yourself. They'll appreciate it and you'll be glad you did it.

Every family has its stray sheep who wander off without telling anyone where they're going, and don't get in touch for ages. And they all have their 'sheepdog' who rounds everyone up and counts them and checks they're OK. Don't resent the fact that you're doing more of the work than someone else. It's the way of the world – and the important thing is that between you all, you manage to keep in touch as much as you can.

And of course you need to be there when they go through tough times. You know that. But what family should really be good at is keeping the support going when everyone else has got bored and moved on. When someone in your family goes through a crisis, they may need support for months or even years. Most of their friends will have forgotten soon after the emergency is over – they have other friends with other crises to attend to – but family are there for the duration. That means you.

Sometimes of course it can mean putting yourself out. Giving up time you had earmarked for something else. Listening on the phone for an hour when you're exhausted and want to go to bed. But that's what looking after each other is all about, and hopefully they'll do the same for you when the time comes.

> # SOMETIMES OF COURSE IT CAN MEAN PUTTING YOURSELF OUT

The more you put out, the more you get back

This is so simple I don't understand why I'm writing it. Except that I meet a depressing number of people who don't seem to have grasped it.

I know this chap who is really gregarious and always has loads of friends. He somehow finds time for them all and manages to make them all feel special. When they're in trouble, he's always there for them. I don't know how he finds the time because he's a working family man. But he always does.[16] He's a good listener and he's very good at making endless cups of tea and handing round biscuits. He even finds time to raise money for local charities too.

A while back my friend went through a really bad patch. His mother died and he lost his job at about the same time. As you'd expect, everyone rallied round with tea and sympathy and offers of help. Oddly though, he seemed surprised. He told me he was hugely touched and couldn't believe that people had been so generous towards him. It seemed perfectly obvious to me. They were sad for him, but pleased to have the chance to repay all the kindness he'd shown them over the years.

I knew another man – elderly chap – who died recently. A nice man, but kept himself to himself. Didn't have much to do with people. I went along to his funeral because he was a neighbour and I wanted to show support for his wife. There were only ten people there, five of them family. I was terribly saddened by that – it seemed so little to show for over 80 years of life.

You know exactly what I'm saying here. The universe doesn't always give you back love from where you gave it. Your generosity

---

[16] He must have been on a time management course I suppose.

to one person may be returned by a complete stranger. But if you keep putting it out wherever you see that it's needed, you'll keep getting it back in buckets.

Of course you're not putting it out because you see it as an investment. People who distribute love far and wide are never doing it because they cynically have their eye on the return they'll get. They're simply doing it because love is its own reward. Yes, I know you want to throw up but I can't find another way of putting it. Despite there being only 24 hours in a day,[17] the more of it you can pass on in the time you have, the more everyone will love you back.

I find it a sobering thought to consider how many people will actually turn up to my funeral when I go. And if ever I suspect it might be fewer than I'd want, I remind myself to put a bit more effort into caring for all the people I love.

> ## THE UNIVERSE DOESN'T ALWAYS GIVE YOU BACK LOVE FROM WHERE YOU GAVE IT

---

[17] *The Rules of Love* Rule 105: Love equals time

THE RULES TO BREAK

By the time *The Rules of Love* was published I was getting a lot of messages from younger readers, many in their early to mid-teens, or still at school or university. I didn't particularly want to put together a book of Rules that were exclusive to this age group, and in any case that would be difficult because – as these readers were telling me – the Rules apply across all age groups. However, these readers were finding many of the books somewhat premature from their viewpoint, such as *The Rules of Management*, or *Parenting*, and I did want to give them something broader that would be as relevant to them as to everyone else.

I'd long been collecting traditional rules which my experience told me didn't actually work, or not reliably – what I thought of as rules to break. You know, things like 'give as good as you get' or 'look after number one'. Collecting these together would be useful to all Rules players and would be really relevant to those younger readers. After all, it takes time – sometimes a lifetime – to build the confidence to follow your own path against the conventional advice. So a book that showed, from real life observation, that it's often better to ignore these so-called pieces of wisdom would really play to these readers along with everyone else.

I would just say that it wasn't difficult to come up with a whole book of these traditional words of sage advice. They're not necessarily rules that should be broken every time, but they are rules that shouldn't be followed blindly because they only apply some of the time. You might argue – certainly I would argue – that in that case they're not actually rules. Suggestions maybe.

When I came to assemble these Rules to break, they didn't seem to group particularly together. I could perhaps have shoehorned them into rough groups, but I couldn't see the point of that if it wasn't going to add anything helpful. So this is the only *Rules* book without sections. Just a hundred Rules not to follow without thinking twice.[18]

Since the book is called *The Rules to Break* each of the 100 chapters is headed up with the rule to break – and ends with the better Rule to follow. However, that would be quite confusing here, as none of the other sections of this book work on that basis. So for our purposes here I've titled the top ten Rules from the book with the actual Rule that works.

There was a huge spread of Rules from this book that were nominated. Top votes went to 'Success is what you say it is' and 'Keep the moral high ground'. Keeping the moral high ground gets a mention in *The Rules of Life* too, and is one of those Rules that I find myself referring to frequently. It's such an essential one for smoothing one's passage through life. One I put a lot of effort into passing on to my kids too.

---

[18] Like this sentence

Success is what you say it is

Rule to break: 'Success is a good job earning lots of money'

People are always ready to tell you that you'll never be successful if you don't do this or that. I'm willing to bet that you've already heard something like: 'You'll never make anything of your life unless you knuckle down and work harder/go to university/pass your exams/get a well-paid job/get a "proper" job.' You know the kind of thing.

But hang on. How are we defining success? And is there only one narrow path that leads there? The parents, teachers or well-intentioned friends who tell you these things are probably assuming what you want out of life is a nice house and plenty of money and a job that commands respect.

Let's set aside for a minute whether they're right about that, and assume it is for now. Is it really true that being good at exams, going to university, landing a job at a prestigious firm and working your way up the corporate ladder is the only way to achieve those material goals? No, of course not. It's one way, but not the only way. There are plenty of real people who've left school early and made a fortune.

But who says that money and an important job *are* the things that constitute success for you? They may be commonly used measures of success, but that doesn't make them right.

The only way to determine what makes for success is to establish what will make you content with your life. And for some people that might mean a flashy car or an impressive job title. If that does it for you, fine, then that's the thing to aim for.

But if it just doesn't feel right, that's because you're one of the many people who are looking for something else in life. Success to you could mean a big family with lots of kids, or a job that leaves you enough time to pursue your other interests, or the satisfaction that you're helping people, or an absorbing job that fascinates you even if the pay is rubbish and the promotion prospects zero.

I know someone who only felt content that he'd achieved what he wanted when he was living self-sufficiently on a wild Welsh hillside with just his dog for company. And someone else who only felt successful when she was able to get a flat in London and live the city life, regardless of the fact that her job was pretty basic and going nowhere. One of my sons is really happy living on a classic boat he's spent years restoring – he's not bothered about how he earns the money to look after the boat. His feeling of success comes from having rescued it and created his own home from it.

Even the people who do hanker after a more traditional idea of success can have widely differing views of it. Some want money to flash it around, others so they feel safe. Some people want a top job for the status, others for the challenge. We're all different. For almost everyone, attaining success will mean hard work and a clear focus. But only you can know what to focus on.

So don't let anyone tell you what it takes to succeed, because they have no idea what success means to you. You, on the other hand, need to think about what it means, or you can't work towards it.

> # HOW ARE WE DEFINING SUCCESS? AND IS THERE ONLY ONE NARROW PATH THAT LEADS THERE?

You're responsible for your own life

Rule to break: 'The world is against you'

Listen, we all get good breaks and bad breaks. People treat us badly, or we get lucky and they spoil us. We all have great teachers, rubbish friends, tricky mums or dads, difficult siblings, supportive adults when we're growing up ... a whole mishmash of influences. Sure, on balance some of us get luckier than others, but we all have negative stuff to contend with. And positive stuff to contend with too.

Once you've left home, however, it's down to you – whoever you are. You can't go around blaming other people for all the bits of your life that aren't how you'd like them to be. It's not your parents' fault, or your school's, or anyone else's. Maybe it was, when you were a little kid, but not any more.

I'm not being unsympathetic. I'm not saying I don't care. I'm just saying that this is how it is. No one else but you can make the rest of your life better. It's no good blaming other people for messing up your childhood, and then going ahead and messing up your own adulthood. If you can't make a decent job of your life yourself, why do you think anyone else should have been able to?

Sometimes blaming other people is the easy option. And yes, maybe you deserve an easy option after what you've been through. But not half as much as you deserve a good life from now on. And that can't happen as long as you put responsibility for your current happiness on the shoulders of your past. You need to wrest control of your life from all of those people who mishandled your childhood, and show them how it *should* be done.

Of course, this means that when you make bad decisions or poor judgements or unethical choices, that's down to you. But, if you're a true Rules player, that won't happen often. When it does, you'll stand up and admit to it – just like all those people who influenced your childhood should have done. Maybe some of them did. You won't blame anyone else, because your life from now on is down to you – the good and the bad.

This isn't just about what's right and fair, it's about what works for you. Have you ever noticed how the people who accept responsibility for themselves are happier? They don't feel out of control, victims of circumstance. Sure, not everything is under our control, and things will go against us from time to time, but if we're in charge, we can take action to put them right – or at least to deal with the aftermath in our own way.

If you blame other people, or events, you're turning yourself into a victim when you could be a winner. The world is full of people who prove this point – if you think about it you'll know plenty of people who have had tough lives but refuse to see themselves as victims, from icons like Nelson Mandela, to some of your own friends. Why wouldn't you want to join them?

> # I'M NOT SAYING I DON'T CARE. I'M JUST SAYING THAT THIS IS HOW IT IS

There's a balance between the right to respect, and tolerance

Rule to break: 'We all have an absolute right to be respected'

My children like to wind each other up – at least when they're feeling frustrated or under the weather or tired. It's what siblings do. Many years ago, we foolishly made it a 'rule' at home that they weren't allowed to do this. If they knew that what they were doing was frustrating one of their siblings, they were to stop. Now, that might seem reasonable to you – it did to me – but of course kids have an irritating habit of subverting rules.

It wasn't long before I'd overhear them saying to each other, 'Stop whistling, it's winding me up. You're not allowed to wind me up'. Or 'It really irritates me when you leave the knife in the butter. If you know it irritates me, you're not allowed to do it'. Yep, that's right, they'd taken our rule and metaphorically scribbled all over it and then jumped up and down on it. Now we found ourselves making another rule to qualify the first one: you have to be tolerant.

Of course it's impossible to stop siblings quarrelling, and indeed you shouldn't try to. It's good for them. But they do like things to be black and white, and this just isn't. The fact is that we do all have a right to be treated with respect, but we also have to temper that with tolerance of other people. Otherwise the whole of life becomes a series of arguments with neighbours, colleagues, authorities, friends and family. And that's before we even start on social media, and people in the wider world who might think differently from you.

OK, so your flatmate never remembers to replace the coffee when it runs out. But come on – they're great company and they keep the place clean and tidy. You can't have everything. Would it hurt so much to replace the coffee yourself? And what about people with different political views from yours? You may not like it, but if you want them to listen respectfully to your beliefs, you have to allow them to express theirs. Respect goes both ways.

It can help to put yourself in other people's shoes here. Are they genuinely doing this irritating thing out of disrespect for you – in which case you have every right to challenge it (diplomatically, I hope) – or are they just being themselves? Do they simply have different priorities or preoccupations to you? Maybe they're being thoughtless, but that's still a long way from deliberate disrespect.

And while you're putting yourself in other people's shoes, think about how you come across to other people. Is it possible that you have any teensy weensy annoying habits? Might you ever irritate other people at all, do you think? Not out of disrespect for them, but just out of seeing the world from your own perspective? We all do it, so perhaps we should be a little more forgiving and tolerant when other people do it to us. Unless they're our brother or sister of course. Then it's everyone for themselves, apparently.

> ## RESPECT GOES BOTH WAYS

It's not morally superior to be tidy

Rule to break: 'A place for everything, and everything in its place'

I was brought up to consider that I 'ought' to get up early, keep my house tidy, say no to chocolate, and plenty of other such beliefs. The adults around me were attaching a moral value to issues which just don't have a moral dimension.

It's tough enough working hard, being nice and trying to leave the world a better place. It's quite unnecessary to load ourselves with all sorts of other spurious standards that just make day-to-day living harder – without benefiting anyone. Why should I have to be tidy if I don't want to, in my own house? Of course I don't drop litter in the street, but I should be free to leave my washing-up until morning. There's no moral issue there. It's not good or bad or virtuous or sinful. It just takes a bit more elbow grease to get it clean if I haven't soaked it, but that's my choice.

Don't let anyone brainwash you into feeling you're at fault in some way if you want to have a lie-in, for example. So long as you don't have to be anywhere else, you can get up as late as you like. It isn't 'good' to get up early. I used to live in a small village where the little old dear lady next door to me would often say, 'I notice your curtains weren't opened until 10 o'clock this morning', in a disapproving tone, as though I was a naughty child.

I had a relative who, whenever you offered her a chocolate, would always say, 'Ooh, I shouldn't ...' and then reach into the box, saying

'It is naughty of me'. No! It's not! It's just a chocolate – eat it if you want to, and not if you don't. But don't get all moral about it.

One of the most frustrating things about some of these false morals is that they become so universally accepted that they can seriously hamper relationships. Very few couples have the same standards of tidiness, for example. That should be fine, and a matter for negotiation over what degree of mess the couple will tolerate in the house, and who will do something about it if it starts to exceed this level. That's quite enough to have to agree on. In fact, however, what almost always happens is that the whole discussion is conducted under the assumption that the tidier person is somehow morally in the right, and the messier partner is inherently wrong. Why? Think it through, and then try to work out why it's any 'better' to be tidy. It may be more practical, or help you find things quicker, or stop you tripping over the furniture. But on the other hand, it's more effort, it's less relaxed and it takes time. Morals don't come into it. It's simply a matter of preference.

Once you start looking out for these things, you may find yourself carrying around all sorts of moral baggage that you don't need. Everyone's parents and teachers impose such values, on top of the genuinely moral ones that they hopefully imbue you with. So question, all the time, and don't let anyone guilt-trip you about things that affect no one but yourself.

> IT'S JUST A CHOCOLATE – EAT IT IF YOU WANT TO, AND NOT IF YOU DON'T. BUT DON'T GET ALL MORAL ABOUT IT

People come and go, and it's OK

Rule to break: 'The best people will be there for you for life'

Ah, if only this were true. The best people may indeed be with you for life – but it could be their life and not yours. The fact is that people die. Some of us learn this brutally as children, many of us are relatively sheltered from it until we get older. Perhaps as children we lose the odd grandparent when their time is up. But sooner or later, we'll lose people who are really close – parents, siblings, best friends, even our own children.

I'm telling you this because if you haven't yet discovered it for yourself, it will come as a horrible shock. Even though of course you know it intellectually, the reality is worse than you can imagine. And it will keep happening, all through your life. There will be lulls, and there will also be years when you feel people are dying all around you. And it won't get any easier to cope with. You may become more attuned to the general idea of it, but each person is precious in themselves, and no easier to say goodbye to for having done it so many times before.

It's other people's deaths that give us a sense of our own mortality. It's hard to believe in your own death, especially when you're young. As people around you die, you start to realise that one day it will be your turn.

But there's one thing that makes all this alright. Yes, really, it is OK. Because new people come along, and they take the place of the people who have gone. I don't mean they replace them, but they occupy a space the same size in our hearts. So as we go through life, we should aim to make room for at least as many new people as there are those who have gone. I never really understood this until I had children of my own. Then I realised that if life stood still, my grandparents, parents and old friends might still be alive, but I'd be missing out on so much – without knowing it – that it wouldn't be worth it.

Of course some individual deaths are never OK, especially those who die young, or those whose deaths affect the very young. But the principle of people dying is worth having if it means that new people are born. You don't have to have your own children for this to make sense – other people's children can bring huge joy into your life (and be a lot less work).

My grandmother had a favourite poem, *The Middle* by Ogden Nash, which she used to recite, and which sums up my point pretty well:

When I remember bygone days

I think how evening follows morn;

So many I loved were not yet dead,

So many I love were not yet born.

> # NEW PEOPLE COME ALONG, AND THEY TAKE THE PLACE OF THE PEOPLE WHO HAVE GONE

RULE 6

You feel what you think

Rule to break: 'You can't help how you feel'

This is a natural follow-on from the last Rule.[19] There are some feelings that you can most certainly help, as we saw. But quite apart from what other people 'make' you feel – or don't – there's a broader principle here.

We all talk to ourselves more than we probably realise. It's not a sign of madness, it's just how people are. Try monitoring your internal conversations for a few days, and listen out objectively for the tone of voice you use.

Some people have conciliatory, forgiving inner voices: 'Never mind, you can't do everything', or 'You may not have found time to call mum, but you managed everything else on today's list'. Others have little slave-drivers in their heads: 'You really should have managed that', or 'Poor mum, it's not fair on her. She'll be feeling abandoned and forgotten and it's all your fault'.

If you spend most of your time being spoken to like this – even by yourself – you'll soon start feeling inadequate and guilty, negative and with low self-esteem. So if you catch yourself doing this, stop and reinvent your inner voice. Start telling yourself how well you're doing (realistically, of course), and cut yourself a bit of slack.

Once again, train yourself to think in positive terms. The moment you catch a negative thought about to form, and before it's put itself into words, overlay it with the thought you'd *like* to have.

---

[19] *The Rules to Break* Rule 51: No one can make you feel anything

Keep on doing this and you'll find within a few days – if you're persistent and relentless about it – that your mood lifts. Just as it would if you were on a long journey and swapped a miserable, doom-laden companion for a positive, sunny one. Which is pretty much what's actually happening.

I've seen people with serious psychological disorders turned around by this approach. It's hard work, but not for very long. It soon becomes habit most of the time and you rarely have to adjust your inner voice any more. Sometimes an emotional trauma can set you back a bit, but you have the wherewithal to get back on track.

Our inner voices have a lot to do with our backgrounds. If you've been brought up by critical parents you're likely to have a more critical or negative inner voice than someone who's been brought up by loving and reassuring parents. But the great news is that, with persistence, this strategy will work no matter how you got where you are.

> # WE ALL TALK TO
> # OURSELVES MORE THAN
> # WE PROBABLY REALISE

Keep the moral high ground

Rule to break: 'Some people are just asking for it'

I've said it before[20] and I'll say it again. There are many times when it's OK to state what your feelings are, but not OK to enact them. I know this is simple to say and really difficult to live up to. I do appreciate that it's tough, but you can do it. It takes a simple shift of vision, from being the sort of person who acts in a certain way, to being a different sort of person who acts in a different sort of way. Look, no matter how rough it gets you are never going to:

- take revenge

- act badly

- be very, very angry

- hurt anyone

- act rashly

- be aggressive.

That's it, the bottom line. You are going to maintain the moral high ground at all times. You are going to behave honestly, decently, kindly, forgivingly, nicely (whatever that means) no matter what the provocation. No matter what the challenge thrown at you. No matter how unfairly another behaves. No matter how badly they behave. You will not retaliate. You will carry on being good

---

[20] In *The Rules of Life*. And I don't apologise for repeating it here.

and civilised and morally irreproachable. Your manners will be impeccable, your language moderate and dignified. There is nothing they can say or do that will make you deviate from this line.

Yes, I know it's difficult at times. I know when the rest of the world is behaving appallingly and you have to carry on taking it on the chin without giving in to your desire to floor them with a savage word, it's really, really tough. When people are being horrid to you it's natural to want to get your own back and lash out. Don't. Once this rough time has passed you'll be so proud of yourself for keeping the moral high ground that it will taste a thousand times sweeter than revenge ever would.

I know revenge is tempting, but you won't go there. Not now, not ever. Why? Because if you do you'll be sinking to their level, you'll be at one with the beasts instead of the angels (see Rule 8), because it demeans you and cheapens you, because you will regret it, and lastly because if you do, then you're no Rules player. Revenge is for losers. Taking and keeping the moral high ground is the only way to be. It doesn't mean you're a pushover or a wimp. It just means that any action you do take will be honest and dignified and clean.

> ## IT WILL TASTE A THOUSAND TIMES SWEETER THAN REVENGE EVER WOULD

RULE 8

Be on the side of the angels, not the beasts

Rule to break: 'No one is perfect'

This fake Rule is too often just an excuse for making bad choices. Of course we don't always get it right, we're not always perfect, but if we follow that as a principle it just becomes a get-out clause.

Listen, every single day of our lives we are faced with an immense number of choices. And each and every one of them usually boils down to a simple choice between being on the side of the angels or the beasts. Which are you going to pick? Or did you not even realise what was going on? Let me explain. Every action we take has an effect on our family, people around us, society and the world in general. And that effect can be positive or negative – it's usually our choice. And sometimes it is a difficult choice. We get torn between what *we* want and what is good for others: personal satisfaction or magnanimity.

Look, no one said this was going to be easy. And making the decision to be on the side of the angels is often a tough call. But if we want to succeed in this life – in terms of how close we get to generating self-satisfaction, happiness, contentment – then we consciously have to do this. This can be what we dedicate our lives to – angels and not beasts.

If you want to know if you have already made the choice, just do a quick check of how you feel and how you react if someone cuts in front of you in a line of traffic in the rush hour. Or when you're in a big hurry and someone stops you to ask for directions. Or if your brother or best friend gets in trouble with the police. Or when you lend money to a friend and they don't pay it back. Or if your boss calls you a fool in front of the rest of your colleagues.

Or your neighbour's trees start to encroach on your property. Or you hit your thumb with a hammer. Or, or, or. As I said, it is a choice we have to make every day, lots of times. And it has to become a conscious choice to be effective.

Now, the problem is that no one is going to tell you exactly what constitutes an angel or a beast. Here you are going to have to set your own parameters. But come on, it can't be that difficult. I think an awful lot of it is self-evident. Does it hurt or hinder? Are you part of the problem or the solution? Will things get better or worse if you take certain actions? You have to make this choice for yourself alone.

It is your interpretation of what is an angel or beast that counts. There is no point telling anyone else they are on the side of the beasts, as they may have a totally different definition. What other people do is their choice and they won't thank you for telling them otherwise. You can of course watch as an impassive, objective observer and think to yourself: 'I wouldn't have done it like that', or 'I think they just chose to be an angel', or even, 'Gosh, how beastly'. But you don't have to say anything.

> # WE GET TORN BETWEEN WHAT *WE* WANT AND WHAT IS GOOD FOR OTHERS

Never say 'I told you so'

Rule to break: 'Let people know when you're right'

Suppose you warn your brother that if he doesn't get his car fixed it will break down. He doesn't do it and, sure enough, it breaks down late at night in the middle of nowhere. Or maybe you advised your friend to leave their job and they didn't listen. Now the firm is going into receivership. Or perhaps your colleague didn't believe you when you said that the company was relocating – and they've just found out you were right. Now, how are you going to respond to all these things, when it turns out you were right all along?

If you're thinking the answer is to say, 'Told you so' then go to the back of the class and stay in after lessons. You can write out 100 times 'I must not say "I told you so"'. But, of course, you're a Rules player, so you won't have been thinking any such thing, will you?

If you're following the last Rule,[21] and not giving anyone advice, this Rule is much easier to stick to. You may privately have foreseen the outcome, but if you resisted proffering advice, well done, and now there's no temptation to say 'I told you so'.

So what's wrong with saying it? Well, the only time the phrase is ever used is when something bad has happened to someone and you predicted it. Or when something good has happened that you predicted and they failed to. So what the expression actually means is, 'Look! I'm right and you're wrong. See?'

Now just explain to me how this is ever a helpful, supportive, kind or considerate thing to say. The fact it's true is neither

---

[21] *The Rules to Break* Rule 73: Don't give advice

here nor there. The fact is you're talking to someone who is at best wrong and at worst also in a hole because of it, and you're choosing to rub their nose in that fact. Is that Rules behaviour? No, it isn't.

When was the last time someone said 'Told you so' to you, and you felt grateful to them, appreciative that they'd drawn your attention to how wrong you'd been in contrast to their own rightness? When did hearing those words cause a warm feeling of love and thankfulness to flow through your veins?

Never, is my guess. Because no one wants to hear it. And I don't blame them. So the next time you're right and someone else is wrong, just button it. *You* know you were right, and that will have to be enough.

> WHEN WAS THE LAST TIME
> SOMEONE SAID 'TOLD YOU
> SO' TO YOU, AND YOU FELT
> GRATEFUL TO THEM?

Don't do guilt

Rule to break: 'Guilt tells you where you're going wrong'

Guilt is a bad emotion, trust me. No, no ... don't start feeling guilty about feeling guilty. I didn't say *you* were bad. I said *guilt* was a bad thing. Some people are overrun with it, almost always because of their upbringing: their religion, their parents, their teachers, some trauma in their past. And I appreciate that it's a very, very hard habit to shake. There's a comfort in it that, like any addiction, makes it hard to give up. But give it up you must, even if it takes you most of your life to do it.

I had a relative when I was younger who used to feel guilty about everything. She felt so guilty she had to talk to her friends for hours about what to do about it. None of which was any help at all to the people she felt she'd wronged, but at least it meant she could talk about herself and how she felt for hours. Because that's what guilt is about: you. It's a way of focusing on yourself that doesn't feel self-indulgent because you're shining a light on the shameful, dark parts of your psyche. Even so, it's sort of a back-handed compliment to yourself because the fact you feel guilty means you care, so you're basically a decent person.

Look, I'm not saying don't ever feel guilty. We all do. But guilt should be just a momentary flash of conscience that alerts you to the fact that you've messed up. It's what you do with the guilt that counts. You feel it (briefly), deal with it and then the guilt is gone. If you really can't deal with it, for whatever reason, then you need to drop the guilt anyway. Because it doesn't help anyone.

If you feel you've treated someone badly, or neglected them, or betrayed a secret, or let someone down, your guilt is in no way helping that person. It can't really, because you haven't got time to worry about them while you're so busy thinking about your own point of view.

I don't want to sound too harsh, because most people who are given to guilt have a complex relationship with it that goes back a long way, and the majority of them are truly not trying to be selfish. On the other hand, I do want to be harsh because – if this is you – you deserve better than to spend so much time berating yourself needlessly. You're damaging your self-esteem and your self-respect, and you need to understand what's going on so you can stop it. Because you really must stop it.

One reason why you must stop is because you need to start thinking about the person or people you think you've short-changed. Go and fix it, before you think about yourself. And then once you've fixed it, you won't need to think about yourself because it will all be OK again. You might *regret* what you did. Hopefully you'll learn from it. But you won't need to feel guilty.

One common factor among people who are prone to guilt is what petty things they feel guilty about. I remember my elderly relative spending hours fretting about the fact that she'd promised to visit a friend and then discovered she had a meeting so she couldn't make it. I couldn't understand why she didn't just phone the friend and say, 'Sorry, my mistake, I've double-booked. How about Wednesday evening?' As an adult I now understand that she couldn't do that. Solving the problem would have deprived her of an excuse to feel guilty, and guilt can be so deliciously indulgent to wallow in, can't it?

THAT'S WHAT GUILT
IS ABOUT: YOU

THE RULES OF PEOPLE

Life would be easy if it weren't for other people. I mean, it would be pretty empty, probably quite boring, certainly less rewarding ... but it would be easier. Most of the problems we encounter are to do with other people, whether we're worrying about them, baffled by them or in conflict with them.

The Rules are all about people. They're drawn from observing people, and they're about how people – you and me – can improve their lives. So it made sense to address the issue of other people head on in *The Rules of People*, and to set out what my people-watching had taught me about how to handle them. We all know people who spend half their lives in conflict, and people who never seem to fall out with anyone. What is it that they're doing differently from each other? And how can the rest of us learn from those people who are loved and respected and seem to get on with everyone without being walked all over?

When I think about all the people I interact with in my life, I realise that avoiding conflict is only one part of what I want to do better. I know that I cope better with challenging behaviour when I understand what drives it. And I realise that some of what keeps me awake at night is wondering how to help the people I love when they're struggling – and beyond that I want to help other people where I can. Then there are the times when I need to persuade people round to my way of thinking, whether it's family, or at work, or other formal settings such as neighbours or local organisations.

So *The Rules of People* has four sections:

- Understanding people
- Helping people
- Getting them on your side
- Difficult people

I'm always slightly uneasy about the term 'difficult people' because by and large people aren't difficult without a reason, and they wouldn't generally see themselves as a 'difficult person' even if they recognise that their behaviour makes your life harder. They generally consider it's justified, and I imagine most of us can be difficult at times. However we all know people that we repeatedly find hard to handle in particular ways, and there are Rules that make it much more possible at least to rub along with them better.

The most nominations here were shared between a few Rules, notably 'Banter isn't teasing'. This is a topic that is becoming ever more widely reported in the media, and it can be hard to navigate. We all enjoy a bit of friendly banter; however, we also know that banter doesn't always feel as we intended to the person on the receiving end. Or maybe that person is us, and we don't know how to say it isn't alright.

People believe what they want to believe

I read something interesting recently. Researchers took two groups of people with opposing political views on a particular topic, and gave them each statistics and other relevant data – hard facts – about it. They discovered that regardless of which side of the argument they were on, people believed that the facts supported their view.

What we believe isn't just about objective facts. It's about our whole outlook on the world, which is a complicated mix of how we were raised, our past experiences, what our friends believe, who we want to impress and how we see ourselves. The whole concept of 'belief' is often applied to spirituality because it has as much to do with faith as with facts. And that's something you can't argue with, however much you might like to.

When was the last time you had a heated political debate with someone who ended up saying, 'Actually, fair point. You're quite right. I've changed my mind'? It almost never happens. Because we all debate the facts, but they're just a tiny part of what makes up our beliefs. For example, a racist and a non-racist arguing with each other will quote loads of statistics about the effect of immigration on the jobs market, or inner-city crime rates, but the data aren't the real reason they hold their view, so that's not likely to change their minds.

What really happens is that we form our beliefs on the basis of a gut feeling, and then we post-rationalise it – we look for facts that back up what we've already decided to believe. Only we're not aware of the process, so we fool ourselves into thinking that our view makes more logical sense than the opposing one. That's why there's really no point discussing politics or religion with other people (apart from people who already agree with you, of course). Problem is, words, facts, statistics – the tools you have to hand when you're debating – will never change people's beliefs.

Frequently, nothing you can do will change them, and you're wasting your time. That doesn't mean it's impossible for someone to change what they believe. But the thing that will change them is an immersive experience. They have to live it for themselves – you can't do it for them.

You might have changed your own beliefs over the years, either suddenly or almost imperceptibly. So look back at why you stopped voting conservative and started voting socialist, or went from being an atheist to a Muslim, or stopped approving of private education, or came to think that abortion should be available on demand, or decided that maybe peanut butter and jam do go together.

How often would you say the change was the result of a discussion with someone who disagreed with your opinion at the time? I'll bet the answer is almost never. It will be because you lived somewhere new, or got to know a group of people whose situation influenced you, or changed your personal circumstances, or did the kind of job that taught you to see the world differently. In other words, no one changed your beliefs for you. You changed them by yourself in response to your own life experiences.

Just remember that the next time you're in a heated debate with someone who holds a view that you consider to be stupid or illogical or untenable in some way. I'm not suggesting you shouldn't stand up for what you believe in. Just be realistic about the chances of getting the other person to change their mind.

> ## THEY HAVE TO LIVE IT FOR THEMSELVES – YOU CAN'T DO IT FOR THEM

Banter isn't teasing

You can argue semantics with me on this one. What one person classifies as banter, the next person might term teasing. Or bullying. Either way, the last Rule[22] was about affectionate and harmless ribbing, while this one is about the territory between what I call teasing and something that is clearly bullying. I'm using banter to mean something that upsets the other person. However, the most obvious feature of this grey area is that the perpetrators have no intent to upset the other person (whereas bullying is sustained and deliberate victimisation). And yet they do.

One of the interesting things about bullying is that it's very hard to assess objectively. Someone at work might say something to you as a jokey put-down, and you might find it amusing and enjoy finding a witty retort. But the same comment from the same person to one of your colleagues might be deeply upsetting. In a scenario like this, it's hard to argue that the person making the remark is a bully. They didn't intend to upset anyone, and yet ... and yet ... well, they have upset someone. Because it's not just what you say, or even how you say it, but also who you say it to.

This is the grey area I mean by banter. And it shouldn't happen, clearly, because someone has been upset and that's never alright. But I didn't call it banter when the comment was made to you – that was affectionate teasing and it's fine. So your workmate is allowed to make this comment to you – but not to their other colleague. Same comment, same commenter, different rules. Confusing, isn't it? The thing is, we all have different experiences and different views of the world. There will be a reason why one person is hurt by a remark that another person would shrug off. Of course, you don't know what that reason is, or indeed how they'll react before it happens.

It means that when you make this kind of jokey, teasing remark, you have to be alert to the other person's response. If you've

---

[22] *The Rules of People* Rule 9: They only tease you if they like you

evidently overstepped the mark and you get the message and don't repeat it, that's the best you can do. If you continue with such remarks, you're straying dangerously close to bullying territory. Yep, you're saying something in the knowledge it will upset the other person. There's no getting round that being bullying. Similarly, anyone – even if they're a friend of yours – who persists with comments once they know they are upsetting someone, is becoming a bully.

The worst cases of banter tend to be among groups of friends, where sustained banter about one of the group can help to cement the 'tribe'. Everyone jokes about how short so-and-so is, for example, because that's become part of the behaviour that identifies you as a member of the tribe. Often almost everyone in the group gets picked on for some characteristic or other. Meanwhile so-and-so wants to stay in the tribe, but actually hates being ribbed about their height. They feel bullied, but don't feel they can say so.

The banter within groups can become a serious form of bullying, where the victim can't express their hurt because this would weaken their membership of the tribe. Yet they don't feel able to leave the tribe. As Rules players, of course, we need to make sure this isn't happening among our friends, never join in, and do our best to put a stop to it. Not easy, but we have to try.

> **ANYONE WHO PERSISTS WITH COMMENTS, ONCE THEY KNOW THEY ARE UPSETTING SOMEONE, IS BECOMING A BULLY**

If they feel small, they'll big themselves up

This is how almost all bullies work. They belittle other people and do their best to turn them into victims. Why? Because a victim is submissive to their aggressor – or, to put it another way, the aggressor is dominant. Bigger, more powerful, more in control. This is the feeling that the bully wants. And why do they want it? Because deep down inside, they feel powerless. Maybe someone else is dominating them, maybe their life feels out of their control, maybe they're secretly scared.

Not only can they feel bigger by making someone else feel smaller, often they also gain (or feel they gain) the respect and admiration of their acolytes – who in fact often surround them in an attempt to avoid being bullied themselves.

People are complicated things. Of course, nothing justifies bullying. But you can sympathise with the reasons behind it without having to condone the bully's way of dealing with them. And although it doesn't make it all alright if you are on the receiving end – or someone you love is – it often helps if you understand where the bully is coming from. And it can help you feel less intimidated if you can see the bully as they see themselves: weak, powerless, victimised.

Obviously this realisation doesn't stop the bullying, it doesn't make everything OK, it doesn't mean the problem goes away. But it can make it a bit less unbearable, knowing that the process isn't even making the bully happy – it's just a symptom of their general unhappiness.

I've encountered a lot of bullies over the years, but I can't recall a truly happy one. The really happy, confident, self-assured, relaxed people I know never bully anyone. Why would they need to? There'd be nothing in it for them.

Sometimes, understanding why someone bullies can be what it takes to resolve things. It's very hard for the person on the receiving end to do this, although not impossible. However, good schools have a high success rate, and a good manager or parent can often sort out such problems in their team or their family. The key is to listen to the bully, find out what is making them feel powerless, and help resolve it. It seems counter-intuitive to help someone who is behaving so badly, but if it makes things better for everyone, it has to make sense. Besides, the bullies often really need help, and we mustn't be blinded by our anger or hurt at their badly chosen approach to helping themselves. No one thinks, 'I'm going to try bullying people – that might make me feel better'. It's an instinctive thing they haven't thought through, and most bullies don't recognise that description of themselves. Obviously – because they see themselves as powerless and victimised, and that's not their idea of a bully.

> I'VE ENCOUNTERED A LOT OF BULLIES OVER THE YEARS, BUT I CAN'T RECALL A TRULY HAPPY ONE

Everyone else is insecure too

Ever had to give a presentation at work? It can be terrifying. Maybe not every time, but they can have a lot hanging on them in terms of meeting targets, impressing the boss, and maybe having an impact on more senior management too. You feel anxious and worried, of course you do, because it matters and nothing must go wrong.

Other people seem to give slick, polished performances and look as confident as if they were just making themselves a sandwich or going for a walk. Nothing to it – done it countless times before. Why would anything go wrong?

It's all an act, you know. Inside, they feel just as nervous as you do. And on the outside, you probably look as calm and self-possessed as them. Why wouldn't they be worried? Their presentation matters as much as yours, so it would be strange if they didn't worry.

Yes, I know there are a few very lucky people out there who are such confident and experienced public speakers that they really don't get anxious. But far fewer than you think. And a handful who don't get as nervous as you do – again, far fewer than you think. Even if you hyperventilate wildly and think you're going to pass out, you're in a much bigger minority than you realise.

And here's another thing. Those people who really do take presenting in their stride – all of them get insecure and nervous in other situations. *Everyone* does. Not all to the same degree, but everyone recognises that feeling. Maybe it's brought on by going to parties, or having to cook for people, or swimming, or job interviews, or committing to a relationship, or spiders, or hospitals, or having sex. We are all a product of our experiences, and no one has had a life devoid of the kind of experiences that lead to feelings of insecurity, worry and anxiety. No one.

If you want to understand people (and that's the way to have the most productive relationships), you need to know that however confident someone appears, they'll have their own insecurities hidden away somewhere. You might never see them, but you can be sure they're there. Sometimes someone you consider to be really together will behave in a totally unexpected way. And maybe it will be because deep down they're just feeling small and anxious. I know people who have a tendency to get angry if they feel under pressure to do something that seems a bit scary to them. Even if they put the pressure on themselves. Some people clam up, or get defensive, or come up with all sorts of spurious arguments against a course of action. They either don't recognise or don't want to admit to their insecurity, but that's what's behind it. So be on the lookout for hidden insecurities, and be kind when you spot them. You know how it feels.

MAYBE DEEP DOWN
THEY'RE JUST FEELING SMALL
AND ANXIOUS

Teenagers hate you because they love you

One of my teenagers voluntarily came over and gave me a hug the other day. As I raised my arms to hug him back he said, 'Get off! Don't touch me'. And there you have the essence of teenagehood in a nutshell.

At the heart of being a teenager is a dilemma. On the one hand, they have an instinctive drive to be independent, and on the other hand they're terrified of being grown-up and want you to go on looking after them forever.

This is why they can simultaneously want you to hug them, and not to touch them – half of them is longing for reassurance while the other half knows it's time to go it alone. It's almost impossible to steer a steady course through the middle of these two con-flicting drives, so they spend a lot of time flipping between the extremes. Some of them can literally fluctuate within moments between telling you they hate you and sobbing on your shoulder in a way they'd never do if they didn't love you. They hate you precisely because they feel their love for you is pulling them back from the growing up they know they have to do.

Here's something I've observed over the years – with only occa-sional exceptions where other significant forces are in play: the kids who find being a teenager the hardest are the ones who have a really strong independent streak, but are also very insecure. They're flip-flopping between the two widest extremes. Those who find it broadly easiest are the ones who are very secure and confident, and not in any particular rush to become independent.

Of course, most teenagers fall somewhere between these two extremes, but you can see the idea. So if you're a parent, you need to help your child to become independent as much as you can. The sooner they acquire adult skills and habits, the sooner they'll recognise that being a grown-up isn't so scary after all, and they can do it. That's why you have to stop making their decisions for them, picking up after them, supplying them with clothes and money, organising their time. Not all at once – you need to step away slowly. Starting from when they're about two.

Becoming a grown-up is emotionally hard work, however much you've been practising since you were young, which is why kids occasionally and suddenly need a hug. And after that they'll rant or grump at you a bit more and let know why you're nothing but an encumbrance in their lives (even though, within another five minutes, they'll be asking you for money, a lift, help with their homework, money, help finding their socks, permission to use the house for a party, and money).

Once they feel they've made it to adulthood successfully, then you can go back to mutually agreed hugging. But first you'll probably have to go through a couple of years when you've no idea from one moment to the next what mood they're in. That's because they've no idea either.

BECOMING A GROWN-UP
IS EMOTIONALLY HARD WORK

Some weirdos are great people

We're all pretty conventional as a social species. We like what we know – of course we do. We feel safe with what we know. And that applies to people as much as situations. You can tell so much about someone from the way they dress, speak, behave, wear their hair. When you meet someone new, you can pretty much pigeon-hole them straight away. You can see what type they are.

So it's quite disconcerting when you meet someone you can't categorise. Someone who stands out as being different. That doesn't feel safe at all. In many ways, the easiest thing is to avoid them if at all possible. Especially if they come across as someone who not only looks odd, but also seems to follow different social rules – you know, they don't get the unspoken stuff about where to stand or when to speak or how to address people.

What's interesting is that it's all to do with fitting in with other people. If you go to places where everyone is like this, suddenly it becomes acceptable, the norm, expected. And then the weirdos aren't weirdos at all. I used to live in Glastonbury, in southwest England, which is where the hippies hang out. A friend of mine once described them as people who 'like rainbow colours, don't brush their hair, and wear all their clothes at once'. They also talk a lot about chakras and healing crystals and how there's no such thing as coincidence[23] because everything is 'meant to be'. If you meet one of these people in Glastonbury – which you will – you don't even notice because they blend into the crowd. But if the same person turned up at an office furniture sales conference, you'd definitely mark them down as a weirdo. Same person, different scenario.

---

[23] Which if you think about it would be the most extraordinary coincidence.

Of course, if you were a hippy working in office furniture, you'd probably save the rainbow clothes for your days off. But all these people are doing is being themselves in every situation, instead of trying to blend with the crowd. Whether it's a deliberate choice or an inability to recognise the effect they have doesn't really matter – the point is that they're simply being themselves. Which is rather refreshing actually, don't you think?

Once you step out of your safety zone and speak to these people, they can be among the most interesting and inspiring people to know. Obviously – as with all people – a few of them might be tedious or not very nice, but it's no more likely than with any other group. Sometimes they have intriguing backstories which shed light on why they appear as they do. Sometimes they're quite brilliant at their jobs. Sometimes they're exceptionally kind. Just like all of us.

If you play it safe and give the weirdos of this world a wide berth, you deprive yourself of the chance to know someone who might be a real positive in your life, in a small way or even a big way. And you miss the chance to learn that stepping out of your safety zone will enrich your life. So what's to lose? Stop avoiding people you can't quite get the measure of, and go and find out first-hand what they're really like and how they tick.

> ## ALL THESE PEOPLE ARE DOING IS BEING THEMSELVES IN EVERY SITUATION

Listen to what they don't say

The last Rule[24] was about helping other people to solve a problem they don't acknowledge exists. This Rule is slightly different, and you might recognise the scenario: the other person is telling you that there is a problem, but however hard you try, you don't seem to be able to fix it.

It's extremely frustrating when this happens. Although it certainly isn't exclusive to relationships, it's most common between partners. In effect, the problem that is being raised is masking a deeper problem. So whatever you do to address the visible problem, you're only ever treating the symptom. You need to identify the underlying cause and treat that.

This can be complicated by the fact that often the other person isn't consciously aware of what's going on either. They may genuinely believe that the symptom they're talking about is the whole problem. Let's give you an example. Your partner complains that you don't do enough housework. So, being helpful and wanting a smooth relationship, you either start doing more round the house, or you rationally talk through why this is difficult (your long hours at work, for example). Your partner agrees, but the problem doesn't go away – or maybe it shifts a bit. Next time perhaps you don't do your share of the washing-up, or tidying the garden, or shopping.

As soon as you realise the problem isn't going away – either it just displaces slightly, or it keeps reappearing despite you thinking you've addressed it – that's the point when bells should go off in your head. Or lightbulbs, because this should be an 'Aha!'

---

[24] *The Rules of People* Rule 42: Learn to be psychic

moment. It should trigger the realisation that the problem your partner is describing is not the real problem.

And generally, the issues in question are like an iceberg. The visible problem is being discussed, but below the waterline there's a much bigger problem lurking. That's your baby. That's the one you need to grapple with.

In the example I've just given, almost always the real issue is that your partner feels taken for granted. And just because you've started vacuuming around occasionally doesn't mean the problem's gone away. You addressed the problem they raised – the housework – but not the underlying cause of the problem.

You see, if your partner feels valued, they won't care who does the most ironing. They'll know you appreciate what they do, and that you're contributing in other ways. The housework thing really isn't the point. You need to consider the whole question of how to help your partner feel valued. That's the biggie. The housework might be one small part of that – but actually, if you can resolve the underlying cause, you may well find it stops mattering who does which bits of cleaning and cooking and shopping.

> ## BELOW THE WATERLINE THERE'S A MUCH BIGGER PROBLEM LURKING

Loneliness is a state of mind

I suspect that, like me, if you think about lonely people you imagine old men and women living on their own. And indeed many old people living alone do feel lonely. However, loneliness in itself isn't about your physical circumstances. It's an emotion, and it has more to do with lacking emotional closeness to other people than lacking physical proximity.

This means that some people can feel happy, fulfilled, satisfied despite very little contact with other people. Maybe because of it. Think of hermits, to take this to its logical conclusion, who are not generally perceived as miserable and lonely, because they have chosen their lifestyle themselves.

On the other hand, it also means that there are people who spend lots of their time in company but who still feel lonely regardless. They might be teenagers or pensioners, shy or gregarious, single or married – it's surprising how many people feel lonely in a marriage that lacks emotional intimacy.

I have one friend who lived on his own for years very happily. Then he met a woman, fell in love and got married. Many years later she died, and he was left alone. He told me that he felt incredibly lonely, despite being in the self-same situation he had enjoyed living in before he met her. I asked him what exactly had changed and he told me, 'I know what I'm missing now'. He had found a closeness with his wife he'd never previously had, and he couldn't stop missing it when she was no longer there.

For a start, this should make it obvious that if someone tells you they're lonely, you won't solve their problem for them by telling them to go and join a club (although I hope by now you won't be telling anyone else what's best for them). There are some people for whom this does the trick, especially if they make close friends over time, but many for whom it doesn't make any sense at all.

Many people find it hard to admit they're lonely. If they manage to admit it, don't be surprised or disbelieving just because they're married, or they've got a big family, or a busy social life, or a job dealing with people constantly. Anyone might feel lonely, regardless of their circumstances.

Equally, given this section is all about helping people, if you have a friend who seems unhappy and you don't know why, consider whether they might be lonely, regardless of their circumstances. Especially if the kids have just left home, or their marriage isn't very happy, or one of their parents has just died.

More people out there than you or I can imagine are lonely, and if we want to help, we need to present ourselves as someone they can really communicate with, not just someone to have a laugh and a joke with – although obviously that as well. Then when they need someone to talk to, and they have the confidence to open up, they'll recognise us as proper friends who can help them feel a bit less alone.

> # IT HAS MORE TO DO WITH LACKING EMOTIONAL CLOSENESS TO OTHER PEOPLE THAN LACKING PHYSICAL PROXIMITY

Credit people with your own ideas

Here's another way to get people on board. I said in the last Rule[25] that people will always buy into their own ideas, so you need to take that and run with it. If you break that down a bit further, you could say that people will always buy into ideas that they *believe* are their own. So logically you should be able to get someone on board with almost any idea, if you can get them to believe that it's theirs.

When this works, everyone wins. You're happy because your idea is the one being taken up. They're happy because as far as they're concerned their idea is the one being taken up. What's not to like?

I should point out that this strategy is a subtle one, and it works best in the early stages of planning. It's no good thinking that you can fall out big time with someone over a clash of ideas, and then suddenly convince them that your idea was really theirs. This is more about identifying people early on who could be dissenting voices and getting them on your side right from the start. Which is always the happiest way to go about things.

I know a chair of school governors who finds this approach invaluable. In a non-executive role, her job is all about trying to find consensus and agreement between a disparate group of people. It doesn't help the school's senior management if the board of governors is disunited. So she brings this strategy into play when there's a strategic decision coming up which she knows one of the governors is likely to resist.

So how's it done? It's all about credit. Once you give someone credit for an idea, preferably in front of other people, it's very

---

[25] *The Rules of People* Rule 62: People generally agree with themselves

hard for them to say, 'That wasn't my idea'. Especially if they're not entirely sure that it wasn't. You can't be heavy-handed about this – you need them to believe it was their idea. So listen out for anything they say that you can pick up on and turn around. Suppose the school is considering expanding, and one governor who is maybe naturally averse to change says, 'Taking on more pupils is going to make the place feel less like a school family and more like a university'. You can respond by saying, 'I quite agree, and actually as our students get older they need to expand their horizons and prepare for university. That's a really good point, thank you.'

Another way of doing this is to tell someone, 'Funnily enough, it was that point you made last week that made me realise what a good idea this was ... ' Or, 'That's a really good idea, and what if we also ... ' You can't put words in someone's mouth, but you can take something they say and develop it into what you'd like them to believe.

Be careful, be subtle, and remember that it only works if they come out of it feeling good about themselves.

> ONCE YOU GIVE SOMEONE
> CREDIT FOR AN IDEA, IT'S VERY
> HARD FOR THEM TO SAY, 'THAT
> WASN'T MY IDEA'

Say thank you properly

We all like to be appreciated. Clichéd but true. Not only that, but people appreciate being appreciated, if you see what I mean, so the act of thanking them will make them want to do their best for you next time. After all, they can be pretty sure their efforts will be noticed and their contribution valued. So everyone wins, because you get what you need from them, and they get to feel good.

There's an art to thanking people. Although almost any thanks is better than none, there are many nuanced ways to say thank you, and finding the best one is a real skill.

The first thing is to get the proportion right. This isn't difficult once you think about it, but it's easy to get wrong if you blunder in thoughtlessly. You don't want to overthank or underthank, do you? You can patronise or embarrass people by making a huge deal out of a relatively minor contribution. By the same token, you don't want to undervalue someone's help by calling out a cursory 'Oh, thanks, by the way ... ' as you leave the room, if they've put in a huge amount of effort and given up loads of free time to you.

And what have they done? Before you say thank you, think this one through. Oh, all right, you don't need to analyse what you're thanking them for every time they make you a cup of tea – but when they've worked hard on a project, or helped organise your wedding, or listened to you moan for days on end, or spent hours researching stuff for you, you need to think it through so you can tell them.

This is at the heart of a really valuable thank you. Let the person know exactly what you are grateful for. Their endless patience? The evenings they gave up? Their attention to detail? Their kindness? Their calmness in a crisis? Say it to them in words – never assume they know. Yes, they know what they did, but they don't know what you valued unless you tell them. Say it or write it, but spell it out.

Now decide how you're going to say thanks. It's not just about what the person has done, but also who they are. Some people much prefer a private thank you. Some will appreciate a personal gift; others might like a card with a carefully worded message. Some will want public appreciation. Don't thoughtlessly give a bottle of wine to a teetotaller, or a bouquet of lilies to someone with hay fever, or throw a surprise party for someone who hates surprises.

An unexpected thank you is worth more than an obvious one. A note or a small gift or a special phone call to say thanks out of the blue are worth much more than the thank you that is accepted as standard, for example thanking the conductor at the end of the school concert. Which means – I hope you'll realise – that you really need to think hard if you're giving a routine thanks to someone who has really earned it, if you want them to feel properly appreciated. It takes a lot to make it sound genuine when you have to say it anyway. The way to do that is to make it as specific and personal as possible, to show you've truly noticed what they've done.

> # THEY KNOW WHAT THEY DID, BUT THEY DON'T KNOW WHAT YOU VALUED UNLESS YOU TELL THEM

THE RULES OF THINKING

We take our ability to think so much for granted that most of us don't even realise we're not making the most of it. If, like me, you collect Rules, it's only a matter of time before you start to notice that a lot of the happiest and most successful people are thinking that bit differently from others. For example, to what extent are the most creative people you know born that way, and how much of it is down to the way they choose to think? I can't answer that question, by the way, except to say that I know it's not all down to genes because I've seen people learn to think more creatively. I've done it myself.

It's not just about creativity of course. Thinking smarter can make you more resilient, healthier, more effective at work and in your wider life, and better at solving problems. It can help you become more organised, and to make decisions more easily. It keeps your brain active and your thoughts healthy. The Rules around thinking aren't tips and techniques, they're about your mindset and how you approach thinking. In many ways they're about removing the barriers to clear thinking, and freeing you up to make better decisions, be more creative and think more healthily.

The great thing about practising these Rules, as I've found for myself by copying those people who seem to be the smartest thinkers, is that it opens your eyes to how much more effectively you could be using your brain, and how much happier, more relaxed, more organised, more collaborative and more effective you can be when you do.

The *Rules of Thinking* is divided into nine sections:

- Think for yourself
- Resilient thinking
- Healthy thinking
- Organised thinking
- Thinking creatively
- Problem solving
- Thinking together
- Making decisions
- Critical thinking

By far the most popular Rule in this book turned out to be 'Be in the present', from the section on healthy thinking. It's a Rule to help reduce anxiety, stress and depression that presumably really worked for those who voted for it.

RULE 1

Take control

When it comes to interpreting what happens in your life, people fall broadly into two camps. Those who believe that it's all down to fate and you can't change it, and those who believe that you have free will and control your own life. Science has not yet agreed which is the case, but it has established that people who believe they control their own lives tend to be happier.

Believing you control your life is crucial to resilience as well. Apart from anything else it motivates you to find ways of coping or at least new ways to think about your problems even where there's little you can do on the face of it. You can't bring back someone who has died, but if you believe your thinking and your decisions will influence the way you deal with it, you're more likely to try to find remedies.

Some people go on quite strict specialist diets when they have a significant illness. You might think it looks like a quack diet and there's no evidence it will make the slightest difference (although of course you're too polite to say so). You might even be right – or you might not. It really doesn't matter. What matters is that by taking control so dramatically, these people are improving their own resilience. So to that degree at least their diet is definitely beneficial.

What's the alternative to taking control? Well, if you feel everything in life is fated and you can do nothing about it, you are painting yourself as a victim when things go badly. And feeling like a victim takes power away from you and leaves you helpless. It does nothing for your confidence and your ability to bounce back.

When things go badly, do something about it. If you can't directly influence events, take control of your response to them. Think differently, choose who you ask for support and how, practise mindfulness or yoga or go for long walks, take some time out – it doesn't matter which of these you do. The thing that really helps is that you are consciously taking charge of your life.

Obviously if there are practical actions you can take that will help, that's great. Your resilience will improve simply because you're in control. So start looking for another job, or lodge a complaint, or get professional advice, or change your diet, or whatever you can think of that will help. It's a double bonus because both the action, and the fact you're taking it, are good for you. You can be as creative as you like. If you think painting your bathroom blue will make you feel calmer, then paint it blue. I know someone who was struggling so much with a job he hated that he left before he became any more miserable. He couldn't find a job immediately so, instead of feeling sorry for himself, he used the time to do the writing he'd always promised himself he would. He never did find another job because his writing career took off instead.

> # PEOPLE WHO BELIEVE THEY CONTROL THEIR OWN LIVES TEND TO BE HAPPIER

Focus on other people

In a way this Rule follows on from the last,[26] because one of the best ways to avoid self-pity is not to think about your own problems too much. Don't sit at home moping, get out there and think about other people's problems instead.

We all have friends and acquaintances who are going through hard times. Think about how you can help, what support they might need. It might be practical or just be a listening ear. You could drive them to their hospital appointment, do their shopping for them, help them with their CV, look after their kids for a day, help get their report written on time. Or they might just appreciate a phone call every week or an evening out so they can talk through their problems.

This is a great distraction for you and a big support to them, and it's so much more than that too. When you help other people, it puts your own troubles in perspective and it makes you feel good about yourself. That builds your self-esteem because you feel worthwhile (rightly) and over time that helps you to feel more positive and better able to cope with your own hardships.

You're not limited to looking around your own group of friends to find someone who needs a bit of bolstering. Lots of people volunteer with charities or other groups in order to focus on other people and be genuinely useful while making themselves feel good at the same time. Almost all of us have some time to do this if we want to. You might have to give up regular visits to the gym, or the odd night out with your friends, or the odd night in with the TV. We can all tell ourselves we have no spare time, but that's usually because we've chosen to fill it up. You can choose how you fill your time and you can give up one thing to make room for another. You have to decide which makes you happier in the long term.

---

[26] *The Rules of Thinking* Rule 18: Think yourself happy

If you decide to do this (and I really recommend it) you can give up anything from an hour a week to as much time as you like. You can pick a role with little responsibility or one with a great deal. You might spend an hour one evening a week helping at a local sports club or put in several days a year as a school governor. You could organise a jumble sale or just help run one of the stalls. You could even find a role where you only help at certain times of year – volunteering at the local half marathon or an old peoples' home Christmas party. The more people-focused the better. It's fine to spend time at home stuffing envelopes for a good cause, but to get the full benefit of volunteering you also need to interact with the people you're supporting.

Remember, this will help you as much as it helps them – it's a win/win. It takes you out of yourself and gives you a huge positive boost that you can then carry over into the rest of your life.

There. See? You haven't thought about your own problems for nearly two pages.

IT MAKES YOU FEEL GOOD ABOUT YOURSELF

Be in the present

Where do you tend to live – past, present or future? Most of us have a tendency towards one or the other, and they all have their pros and cons. Even if you are inclined to live in the present, however, you tend to do it unconsciously most of the time.

There's a good deal of research to show that if you practise what is known as 'mindfulness' it can reduce anxiety, stress and depression. In part this is because you are more likely to become aware of these feelings sooner so you can address them before they become entrenched. Mindfulness in its basic form is an exercise you set aside some time each day to do. However the greatest benefit is that – like other thinking styles – the more you do it, the more of a habit it becomes, until you incorporate it into other parts of your life too, and slip in and out of it whenever it's helpful.

Essentially you need to set aside a few minutes each day. This might always be the same time and place or you might vary it. Whatever works for you. You're aiming to make this a habit though, so bear that in mind. It doesn't have to be quiet or peaceful, so long as you don't have to interact with your surroundings for the duration. So a park bench or the train to work are fine. If sitting still is difficult, you can go for a mindful walk.

Now comes the tricky bit, and it will be tricky at the beginning, but it will become easier and easier the more you do it. Just focus on the present moment and take the role of an observer. Notice what's happening while remaining detached from it. Don't judge. Notice that your left foot is slightly uncomfortable or that there's birdsong nearby. Notice your thoughts without judging them.

Whoops, yes, that was the really tricky bit I mentioned. You're not aiming to empty your mind, as you might if you were meditating, but you don't want to get caught up in thoughts and emotions either. You *will* get caught up, I can tell you now, at least until you've had plenty of practice. That's normal, but whenever you notice you've been distracted by your thoughts, just bring yourself back to observing them without being sucked in.

This very tendency to get carried away by your thoughts demonstrates the point of mindfulness. We spend most of our time in this state, controlled by our thoughts and feelings, and mindfulness is a valuable exercise because it separates out our underlying self from our responses and reactions.

It doesn't matter if you have lots of thoughts or worries while you're being mindful, so long as you observe them. 'Ah, yes, here's some anxiety about tomorrow's presentation.' 'Hmm, this looks like my usual worry about social situations.' Stand back and look at your thoughts – don't get involved, don't try to fix them.

> ## STAND BACK AND LOOK AT YOUR THOUGHTS – DON'T GET INVOLVED

RULE 4

Think outside your head

It's very hard to operate effectively and efficiently when your head is cluttered. You're so busy trying to hold onto those important thoughts, there's barely any head room left for thinking through the current task. And you keep catching yourself short, thinking, 'Oh, I must remember to call so-and-so ...' or 'Oops, I need to check we have enough of those . . . ' or 'Actually this will need to be done before Thursday ...' All those thoughts jostling for space make it much harder to focus on the task in hand. Either you forget things or you keep jumping from one thing to the next without finishing anything properly. Or both.

If you're running a big project at work, or organising a local event, or launching into a house move, you'll probably make yourself some notes. But it's not enough to write down some of the things you need to do – you need to write them all down. Yep, everything. Every last tiny thing.

I used to do a job that was essentially project management, and I never went anywhere without a spiral-bound notebook and a pen shoved into the spirally bit. If anyone mentioned a task – however small – I jotted it down. If I suddenly remembered something I had to do, or remind someone else to do, down it went. I kept it by my bed at night so I didn't lie awake worrying I'd forget things come the morning. At the end of each day, I went through my notes and tidied them up. You don't have to have a spiral-bound pad. You can diarise things, email yourself (or other people), cover your desk or fridge in sticky notes, whatever works for you.

The really important thing to grasp here though is not a handy tip about writing things down, useful though that certainly is. What you have on your notepad (or diary, or sticky notes, or shopping list, or the back of your hand) is only one part of it. Yes, it gives you an efficient system for not forgetting things. But the really important stuff is what goes on inside your head: nothing. Space.

Free working memory. Clarity. Lovely, easy, relaxing emptiness. So now you can deal with each task on its own, *without stress*, because you've moved all the other clutter out of your head and onto a piece of paper. If anything else invades your head space, just move it on. Externalise it. De-clutter your brain.

Here's another thing worth writing down – every time someone is supposed to get back to you on something, make a note. Diarise it, or keep it in 'sent items', or have a place for it, so when they don't get back to you, you have a system that means you'll remember to chase them. Imagine how much thinking space that will free up.

I clear my emails every day. That way my inbox contains only items I need to action, and my sent items contain only things I'm waiting on other people to respond to. As soon as they do, the sent item gets archived. Yes, it sounds ridiculously over-organised to some people, but you know what? I don't care what they think. What I care about is that I don't have to remember any of those things because my inbox or my sent items are doing all my remembering for me, and I can keep a clear head.

> ALL THOSE THOUGHTS
> JOSTLING FOR SPACE MAKE IT
> MUCH HARDER TO FOCUS ON
> THE TASK IN HAND

RULE 5

Loosen up

I remember a group discussion at work where we were supposed to be brainstorming ways to help our staff feel appreciated. The idea with brainstorming, of course, is that all ideas are welcome as a jumping off point and now is not the time to be negative. One member of the group, however, responded to almost every suggestion negatively. His favoured expressions were, 'That wouldn't work' and 'We've always done it this way before'. When I asked him for ideas of his own he didn't have any.

For some reason this sticks in my mind because it was one of the most extreme examples I've seen of this kind of inflexibility. The colleague in question simply couldn't see beyond his current mindset and was unable to imagine solutions he'd never actually experienced. He was as keen as the rest of us to recognise the hard work our people had put in during a tough year – it wasn't that he didn't agree with the aim – but his thinking was so rigid that he was unable to let go of his preconceptions about how things should be.

This is just no good if you're serious about being a Rules thinker. You have to let go, loosen up, embrace change and difference and new ideas. Of course not all of them will be workable, but you have to be open to those that will.

I'll promise you one thing. If you only ever do what you've done before, you'll get nowhere. You'll stagnate, shackled to the past, bogged down in routine. At the best of times this might suffice, but it closes off countless possibilities for making things even better. When things are bad, rigid thinking will prevent you finding ways to dig yourself out of the mess. Whether your problems are financial, relationship, lifestyle or work-based, you can't afford to limit yourself like this.

The world changes. The pressures on you, at work or at home, will be different from what they were last year. So not only are the old solutions no longer necessarily the best, they may not be viable at all any more. Fifty years ago, if you needed to get a message to someone urgently, you sent them a telegram. Well, that doesn't work any longer. Fortunately, however, some innovative people who were open to new ideas came along and invented texting.

Yes, I know that's an extreme example to make my point, but we didn't switch from telegrams to texts overnight. Some people held out against technological change for longer than others, wanting to keep doing what they'd always done, and they slowly fell behind. Until, in the end, they had to change their ways. You and I, though, we don't want to be the last to catch up. We want to be ahead of the game, solving problems in the best way possible, not in the least bad way from a limited menu of ways we've managed before. We want to have a full portfolio of options without restricting ourselves needlessly.

So from now on, outlaw phrases such as 'It's how we've always done it', whether out loud or even just in your head, so you can resist the kind of rigid, inflexible thinking that makes it impossible to solve problems effectively.

> WE WANT TO BE AHEAD OF THE GAME, SOLVING PROBLEMS IN THE BEST WAY POSSIBLE

Don't settle for your first answer

Most problems have more than one solution. If I'm wearing a coat and the weather heats up so I start sweating, I could cut the sleeves off the coat to cool myself down. It's *an* answer, but that doesn't make it the best one. If I thought about it for a bit longer, it might occur to me to remove the coat.

Your money problems, or your work dilemma, or the fact you and your kids keep shouting at each other, or the question of what to do with your mum now she can't really live alone any more, also have more than one solution. And the best one won't necessarily be the one you think of first.

The first answer you come up with is really useful, mind you. Having a plan B is fantastic for taking the pressure off, which frees your mind up to think more creatively. So definitely make a note of any solution you think of, until a better one materialises. Even if that better one still only really warrants becoming the new plan B.

Listen, it can take time to come up with a really good answer to your problem. Don't expect it to be instant or you'll assume the instant answer is the best one. That's a recipe for muddling through life. Every time you hit difficulties, you take an option that's good enough but no more. Is that really how you want to live? Do you think that's the route to success and happiness?

Sure, when the problem is a minor one, it may not matter that much. But remember, we're getting into good thinking habits. If you train your mind to think the best way every time, it will think the best way when it really matters. And the best way to think is the one that leads to the best – not the quickest – outcome.

So how do you know when you've found the real, best solution? There's no simple answer but there are pointers. You're looking for the one that ticks the right boxes – not just the most boxes, but the ones that matter most. So for example, when you're deciding what to do with your elderly mum, her happiness is (I hope) an essential box to tick. Solutions that don't provide for this aren't going to make the grade. You'll need a list (mental or physical) of the essential components of a good solution, and also the preferable ones.

And adopt this principle: whatever solution you come up with, say to yourself, 'That's a good starting point. Now where can I go from here?' In other words see every idea as a beginning and not an end point. Always look for ways to develop your first thought into something even better. Assume it can be improved on. Just don't let this take you down a one-way tunnel. Remember there might be other ideas, other jumping-off points, that would take you in a different direction and that are also worth considering. If there's room for improvement, it can't be the best solution yet.

Sometimes, if you're lucky, you'll just *know* when you find the right solution. Even so, although it might feel like a gut response, your gut will have been informed by the thinking you've done before. That's how it recognises the right answer when it sees it.

> ## SEE EVERY IDEA AS A BEGINNING
> ## AND NOT AN END POINT

RULE 7

Facts are neutral

You need to avoid all the pitfalls of sloppy thinking, and that means you need to be on the lookout for them. These are the little errors that make us believe our thinking is sharper than it is. We don't want to feel smart, we want to *be* smart. We want to spot the traps so we can take avoiding action before we fall into them.

I've mentioned before that one of the big errors of thought is believing that the facts, the data, the stats are backing up your own viewpoint. This is known as confirmation bias, when you search out information that supports your argument, or interpret the facts that you're presented with as backing you up. It's a very comfortable thing to do – it makes you right, and saves you the effort or loss of face of changing your mind. All nice and simple.

Unless you're a Rules thinker. Smart thinking isn't always comfortable or nice. Sometimes it means re-evaluating our beliefs or changing our whole approach to a subject. That's the price you pay for being a top-class thinker. No more 'nice and comfortable' for you.

Look, facts aren't interested in helping you. They don't want to back you up, support you, corroborate your thinking. They're just facts, OK? Sometimes they might happen to reinforce your point and sometimes they might refute it. That's the way they are. What you have to do is be dispassionate about working out what they mean, because they won't tell you that. It's not their job.

Suppose I survey a thousand people and I ask them what their favourite breed of dog is. Let's imagine the highest percentage of people – 8 per cent – vote for Labradors. That is a fact (in my imaginary world) and it's not trying to tell you anything. It just is.

Along comes a Labrador lover who is delighted, but not very surprised, to learn that more people favour Labradors than any other breed. That's what they always thought – of course Labradors are best. But what's this? A Labrador hater[27] is looking at this data and is feeling thoroughly vindicated. Just what they thought! Fewer than 10 per cent of people favour Labradors. Ninety-two per cent of people didn't put them first.

So who is right? On one level, of course, they both are. They're both reading the data correctly. But they're interpreting it very differently because they're both falling into the trap of confirmation bias. See how easy it makes things for both of them – no need to wonder if perhaps they've been wrong up to now, no need to rethink whether other people really share their views on Labradors, no need to lose face in front of other Labrador lovers (or haters – yeah, them).

Look, you have to question your interpretation of the facts, interrogate your own thinking process, if you're going to get to the truth of anything. It may not always be pleasant, but it has to be done.

SMART THINKING ISN'T ALWAYS
COMFORTABLE OR NICE

---

[27] I know they're not really a thing. Actually I'm starting to go off my imaginary world . . .

Spot the box

Lots of people will exhort you to 'think outside the box'. There are plenty of strategies for doing so and lots of them are great, productive, really helpful. What most of them fail to do, however, is to identify or describe the 'box' you're supposed to be removing yourself from.

In broad terms of course we know what it is. The box represents rigid thinking along the usual furrows that will lead to the same places those furrows always lead to. But what is it specifically – in terms of the individual project or creative exercise you're engaged in right now?

The answer to that question is going to be different every time. But do you ask it? That's where the strategies seem to be missing a page, and it's an absolutely crucial question. It's hard to describe how much easier it is to think outside a box when you know where the box actually is. So make that your starting point.

This works really well in business because it gives you a competitive edge. All the local retail bakeries round my way (and yours, I'd guess) are in towns – that's where all the people are, so if you want to open a bakery with maybe a café attached, you open it in the middle of town. But a couple of years back someone here decided to think outside that box: they opened a bakery, with a café, on a small out-of-town trading estate. Not enough units on the estate itself to keep the business going, so you might not have great hopes for the business. However, it's now the best-known bakery in the area and the café is regularly packed. Why? Apart from the great food, parking is way easier on the trading estate than it is in town, so it's a much better place to meet up. Those bakers spotted the 'be in town' box and climbed out of it.

Don't forget that you might be thinking inside several boxes at once (I don't really know what that looks like – I suppose they must be like Russian dolls). Maybe you're trying to design a wedding reception in your village hall. So there's a box you're stuck in that says 'village hall' – maybe you could hold it somewhere else? But hang on, you're also in a box that says 'wedding reception'. Try thinking outside that one too. And of course there's a box marked 'getting married'. Of course you might still end up getting married and having the reception in the village hall. But you could elope, or get married and take everyone for a slap-up meal afterwards, or go to a registry office with two friends, then have a honeymoon (that's a box too, of course), and then throw a big party for everyone when you get back. Or not.

Just because you've got out of the box, it doesn't mean you can't climb back into it again if you choose to. But at least take a peek outside and decide if you really like the box or if you were just thinking inside it because it was there. You see, even if you get back into the box, your horizons will be wider for having spent a bit of time outside it. The box has become transparent now you know what's beyond it. And the chances are that the ideas you generate will be more creative, interesting and exciting than if you'd sat firmly and blindly inside it from the off.

> # IT'S HARD TO DESCRIBE HOW MUCH EASIER IT IS TO THINK OUTSIDE A BOX WHEN YOU KNOW WHERE THE BOX ACTUALLY IS

Feed your mind

Einstein is a bit of a hero of mine, and he reckoned that imagination was more important than knowledge. That's even more true now when almost all knowledge is out there in the ether waiting for you to call it down at the tap of a keyboard. You really don't need to be storing it in your head. But imagination – you can't download that, and imagination is the key to creative thinking. So what you really need to do is expand your imagination any way you can.

Einstein also said the way to have intelligent children was to read them fairy tales. To increase their intelligence further, you should read them more fairy tales. When you hear the words of a story, the plot might be provided for you by the writer, but your imagination supplies the pictures. When you read it to yourself, your imagination supplies the voices and the sounds too.

Do me a favour – go and read the prologue to Shakespeare's *Henry V* if you don't already know it (it's out there in the ether waiting for you). He describes perfectly what the imagination is capable of and how you can use it to imagine even, for example, that the confines of the theatre 'hold the vasty fields of France'. The human imagination is an extraordinary thing, and it's almost a sin not to make our own as strong and agile and vivid as we can.

Reading fiction is essential. And, incidentally, Einstein's point is important if you want your children to develop brilliant creative minds. Read to them as often as you can and give them a love of books. It's no good just watching a movie, where all the imagining is done for you. That's great, but it's an entirely different thing and no substitute for reading. And encourage them to make things up. Small children will believe in magic, and in Santa, and the tooth fairy, for years if you help them. I had friends whose children firmly believed that the family cat could actually fly, and it was a delight to find that their parents had sensibly allowed them to continue in this belief, where many parents would unthinkingly have said, 'Don't be silly. Cats can't fly.'

If I had to put one activity at the top of my list for developing the imagination that you need in order to think creatively, it would be reading. Fortunately, however, I don't have to put one thing at the top, and there are lots of other ways to feed your creative mind. Reading poetry, writing anything, music of whatever kind you enjoy (and remember to shake things up occasionally – don't get stuck in a rut). Plenty of very clever comedians, especially the more surreal ones, force your mind to make unexpected leaps and twists and jumps, and knock your thinking out of its ruts, along with comedy shows from Monty Python onwards.

If you think about it, loads of jokes are based around catching your brain unawares, setting up a pattern and then unexpectedly breaking it. And immersing yourself in this kind of humour, hanging out with friends that make you laugh, watching funny shows, is one of the most enjoyable ways to encourage your mind to think more creatively.

WHEN YOU HEAR THE WORDS OF A STORY, THE PLOT MIGHT BE PROVIDED FOR YOU BY THE WRITER, BUT YOUR IMAGINATION SUPPLIES THE PICTURES

Untangle the knots first

Some decisions are especially complicated because they're inter-woven with other decisions. You don't know what to do about A until you've sorted out B, but B is dependent on C. Sometimes they intermesh so that you've no idea where to start, let alone what to decide. One couple I know was trying to decide whether to move to London (150 miles away), where to send their child to school, and she was considering cutting her working hours to free up time to retrain. And if so, what should she retrain as? They couldn't see how to make any of these decisions until after they'd made the others. This kind of knotty problem often leads to stall-ing and procrastination,[28] simply because it's so overwhelming.

However, if you muster all your thinking skills you *can* untangle this kind of knotty problem. Trust me. First of all, put any of the elements you can into series. There may be no point thinking about where to send your child to school until you know where you'll be living. If you don't move to London, the options for retraining will be limited by what courses are available locally so, again, the 'London or not' decision needs to come first.

Not only will this clear things a bit, it will also show up whether you need to reprioritise. Perhaps, when you look at it like this, you'll realise that your choice of school is really important to you, and you don't want it to be reliant on where you live – you'd rather fit your location around the school, not the other way around.

Good. You're making headway. Some decisions are on hold until you know where you're living and you've gained a sense of pri-ority about the decisions that will come first. Suppose this train of thought made you realise that the choice of school is the most important thing. That has now become a parameter for your other decisions: must be near a suitable school. Maybe even a specific school – in which case the location issue is solved too.

---

[28] Let's deal with procrastination later. It can wait . . .

OK, that all helped, but there are still some interlinked decisions left. So the next thing to do is to think through each one in isolation. Suppose – for the sake of argument – the other complications weren't there. In an ideal world, what discipline would you want to retrain in? It's much easier to think this through when your head isn't cluttered with all the other stuff. It may be that you don't end up with your ideal solution, but I can't emphasise enough the importance of knowing what that ideal answer is. That way you'll make a conscious decision – on the balance of benefits – about how far you're compromising on it.

You should find that by the time you've gone through this sequence – put the decisions you can into series, prioritise those you can't, then think through each in isolation – everything will start to become clear. My friend did this and realised that she'd nearly made a decision she'd have regretted (retraining in a discipline because it was available, not because she really wanted to do it). Separating out the thinking process had given her the clarity she needed.

> IT'S MUCH EASIER TO THINK
> THIS THROUGH WHEN YOUR
> HEAD ISN'T CLUTTERED WITH
> ALL THE OTHER STUFF

THE RULES OF LIVING WELL

I'd always planned to put together the Rules I'd collected about health into a book. I'm not quite sure why it didn't happen earlier. My publisher and I had a lot of conversations about the title – we worried that *The Rules of Health* would sound too focused on physical health, and we knew we wanted to include all the important Rules I'd observed over the years about emotional and mental health too. We came to the conclusion that *The Rules of Living Well* encapsulated what these Rules were all about – everything from relaxation and confidence to exercise.

As always, there's nothing in the book about what you should eat or which exercises you should do. These Rules are ones that healthy people follow in terms of attitudes and mindsets. As well as sections on resilience and food, I also included sections on aspects of your life such as learning and retirement, in order to cover all the Rules I'd amassed about staying healthy in mind and body.

I ended up with ten sections altogether:

- Balance

- Confidence

- Resilience

- Exercise

- Relaxation

- Food

- Learning

- Parenthood

- At work

- Retirement

- Challenge

The section on challenge is about how to survive crisis and trauma. Very few of us escape these during our whole lifetime, and the Rules I'd seen put into practice can make a huge difference to how you get through. No point knowing how to live well when times are good – that's the easy bit. *The Rules of Living Well* needed to give some guidelines for coping when the going gets tough.

The highest number of votes here was for one of the Rules in this section: 'Forgive and don't forget'. It's a useful Rule on an everyday level, but essential for your wellbeing if you've been through a devastating divorce, say, or an abusive childhood. It's not easy, but it's what you deserve. I know that once I'd seen it in action, and then learnt to adopt it for myself, I started to live a whole lot better.

RULE 1

It's not all about you

OK, time to level with you. I know this book is called *The Rules of Living Well* but the last thing you need is to focus on yourself. That's my job, and this is the first of 100-odd Rules that are chosen to help you feel as good as possible. You, however, need to think about yourself less.[29]

I'm not trying to give you a hard time, to tell you off for putting yourself first, to criticise you for having an ego. I'm trying to help you. The fact is that people who think about themselves all the time are rarely happy. That's not just my opinion – research has shown it too. And when you consider it, that's hardly surprising. When you focus on yourself (or anything else) you're bound to start noticing the bits that aren't as you'd like – the qualities, the money, the relationships you wish you had. No one's life is perfect, and there will be things you can't change, or at least not now. The more time you spend thinking about those shortcomings, the more importance they will take on in your mind, the more touchy you'll be when you think you've been slighted or treated unfairly or overlooked.

We all know these people. They talk about themselves constantly, and if you try to steer the conversation elsewhere they just bring it back to themselves. They see everything as being about them – their boss rearranged the rota in order to punish them or get at them or make their life more difficult for some reason. Never because it was simply a more efficient system. Never because the boss wasn't thinking of them at all, but trying to balance lots of people and priorities. They can't conceive that their boss wasn't considering them personally, because they think of themselves all the time, so they have no grasp of a universe in which they're not at the centre.

---

[29] How you square that with reading this book is your problem.

Look, I want you to have the best life possible, and of course that won't work if you never consider your own needs and wants. But to stay in balance you need to make sure you don't constantly turn your eye inwards on yourself. Understand where you fit into the bigger picture, into the rest of the world, and keep your focus outwards. That's actually where all the good stuff is.

And here's a phrase I hate: 'me-time', or 'for me'. All your time is me-time, 24 hours a day. Why aren't you spending all of it doing the things you want to? You might not enjoy them all, but in the end you do them because you want to – I dislike housework, but I don't want to live in a pigsty. I don't enjoy my kids' tantrums, but I love being a parent and the tantrums come with the package. I've had jobs I hated, but I wanted the money. I could have changed jobs, or lived on the streets, but I was choosing not to. My time, my choice. The concept of time for relaxing – which I think is behind the phrase 'me-time' – is fine in itself. Part of the problem with the phrase is that it implies the rest of your time is less good, is somehow *not* your choice, which makes it much harder to embrace all your other activities, and to acknowledge that you chose them too.

Alongside that, the phrase implies that you are more important than everyone else in your life, and the best time should be saved for your personal indulgence. That sounds to me dangerously as though the balance has slipped and you're sneaking towards centre stage. It might look inviting, but it won't make you happy.

> # TO STAY IN BALANCE YOU NEED TO MAKE SURE YOU DON'T TURN YOUR EYE INWARDS ON YOURSELF

Your feelings are your own

Your level of confidence is largely about how other people see you – or rather, your perception of how others see you. You may not even be right about it, and indeed many people with low levels of confidence assume other people see them as stupid or useless or unattractive or incapable, when in fact that may not be what people are seeing at all. So you're judging yourself on your judgement of other people's judgement – and that's a pretty flimsy reason to feel insecure about yourself. Besides, they're probably not judging you at all – just worrying about what *you* think of *them*.

The trouble comes from allowing these supposed opinions to influence the way you feel. Even if someone tells you that you're rubbish at your job, or a bad parent, you don't have to agree with them. One friend of mine is a brilliant interior designer. If you query a design scheme of hers she'll confidently explain to you exactly why it *will* actually work. But if you were to question the way she raises her children, she'd feel miserable and inadequate. Why? Because she's confident about her work but not about her parenting skills. So that's about her, not about the other people. Many of us have this mis-match of confidence levels between different areas of our life.

You are responsible for your own feelings, no one else is. It's what you think that matters, not what they think. Whether this is a specific lack of confidence, say as a parent or at your job, or a more generalised lack of social confidence, you need to focus on your own view of yourself, independent of what anyone else thinks or says.

So ignore everyone else and decide for yourself whether you're as good at your job as you'd like to be. If not, don't feel miserable and insecure: do something about it. Think it through, adopt new strategies, ask for help, do some training, change jobs if you want to – get yourself to a point where you *know* you're good at your job, and then take responsibility for feeling confident and secure about it. Don't rely on anyone else to guide how you should feel.

That approach – identifying any shortcomings and putting them right – applies to being socially confident too. If you want to feel more self-assured, you'll have to work at it. Don't decide you're no good at it and never will be. You can teach yourself social confidence, by learning ploys and strategies, putting yourself just slightly outside your comfort zone until that feels OK and you're ready to expand the zone further.

It can also help to consider why you lack confidence. Sometimes it's rooted in the past, in the things your dad used to say to you, or the way you were bullied at school. Now you're a grown-up you can step out of those shoes and into more self-assured ones that fit you better. It's much easier to do this consciously, after analysing the root of your social insecurity.

By the way, you may already have worked out that if you can't rely on other people's poor opinions of you – real or perceived – you can't rely on their good opinions either. If people pay you compliments or admire you or show you respect that's all very nice, and I expect you'll enjoy it, but don't ever let it be a substitute for your own honest appraisal of yourself.

> # IT'S WHAT YOU THINK
> # THAT MATTERS, NOT WHAT
> # THEY THINK

Train your mind to relax

The human mind is an extraordinary thing. The more you use and reinforce those neural pathways, the stronger they get. In the same way you've learnt to salivate when you see or smell food, so you can train your mind to relax in response to certain things.

So if you routinely relax your mind by closing your eyes and taking deep breaths, or by playing patience, or by going for a five-minute walk, your mind will learn to relax when it receives these triggers. Once you've trained your mind to associate these ploys with relaxing, it will get the message and drop into relaxation mode pretty quickly as soon as you start.

If you think about it, it will be much easier for your mind to relax in response to these activities if it's not very stressed to begin with. No, bear with me, that's not as stupid as it sounds. Clearly strategies that only reduce your stress when you're not feeling stressed in the first place are of questionable use. But think about it: if you're training your body to run a marathon, you start by running just a few kilometres and then build up. In the same way, if you train your mind to relax when it's easy, it will start learning to associate those same actions with relaxation even when you are under pressure.

So don't gloss over this Rule on the grounds that you're not stressed at the moment. Good! Perfect timing! Now is exactly the moment when you should be establishing these techniques so that they really work when you next need them. And it's only a matter of time – sadly all our lives go through stressful episodes, sometimes for a prolonged period. Whether a member of your family is seriously ill, or your job is on the line, or your relationship is falling apart, or you can't make your mortgage repayments, there will come a period of weeks or months, maybe more, when everything you can do to keep your anxiety or fear in check will be precious.

Of course when that time comes it will be great if you can spend as much time relaxing as possible. Holidays or open-air trips or evenings with friends or trips to the gym, they'll all play a part. However, those frequent little moments throughout the day will keep pegging back the stress to a manageable level, and keep you going between the more dedicated periods of relaxation. But only if your mind is trained for it, and can short-cut straight to relaxation mode almost the moment you start.

This is also useful if you need to relax quickly just ahead of some activity. For example if you regularly compete in some kind of sport and get anxious just beforehand, or maybe find it nerve-racking giving a presentation and want a quick technique you can use immediately before you start. Those are the moments when there isn't time to take a few minutes to get into the mood. You want your mind to relax automatically as soon as it gets the signal.

> ## ALL THOSE LITTLE MOMENTS OF RELAXATION THROUGHOUT THE DAY WILL KEEP PEGGING BACK THE STRESS TO A MANAGEABLE LEVEL

Zen it

Here's a lesson I learnt like a thunderbolt from someone else, and it came as a huge surprise after decades of being intermittently stressed and frustrated about various and random things, as most of us are. Well it may surprise you to know that most of that stress is optional. There's simply no need for it. You can just turn it off.

Yeah, me too. I didn't believe it at first. All those years of getting stressed by slow traffic, and difficult colleagues, and exams and interviews, and computer malfunctions, and the hot water running out just as I got under the shower. All wasted. I didn't need to get stressy about any of it. I just wish someone had explained that to me sooner.

It wouldn't be putting it too strongly to say that it's changed my life. I've become calmer than ever before, and that adds to my enjoyment of every single day. And all because someone told me that I didn't have to get stressed – it was a choice I was making and I could stop making it.

That was the epiphany – the realisation that I was choosing it, albeit entirely unconsciously. If the traffic is slow, it's slow. Nothing I can do about it. But here's a choice I do have: be stuck in slow traffic feeling stressed, or be stuck in slow traffic feeling calm. No prizes for guessing which of those is preferable.

When we feel stressed by these everyday irritations, we have an internal conversation about how irritating it is, and how we'll be late, and how we already have too much to do, and how this will throw the whole day out . . . but none of those escalating, frustrated thoughts will speed the traffic up. So why think them? Just dump it. Turn up the radio, sing along, and think about something else.

The language around stress and frustration isn't helpful, and is a lot of why it never dawns on us that we have a choice. We say, 'the traffic stressed me out' or 'my colleague is driving me mad' as though *they* have the control and they're visiting the frustration upon us. It makes us victims. And no one ever explains that actually we *chose* to be frustrated by the traffic, or we *let* our colleague drive us mad. And if no one tells you that, why would you ever stop feeling stressed by these things?

I appreciate that for people with real anxiety issues this Rule isn't going to turn everything around in a moment. And indeed if you aren't hugely anxious but for some reason you want to continue getting stressed, you carry on. It's no one's problem but yours, and if you don't see it as a problem that's great. I'm just trying to help if, like me, you've spent a lifetime feeling intermittently stressed and would quite like to stop now.

Since I learnt this Rule I've successfully applied it to everything from a car break-down to moving house – yes it even works for big stuff. The only thing I haven't managed to apply it to is those rare occasions when I'm seriously anxious about someone I love – not minor concerns (it still works for those), but real long-term health worries. There's too much deep emotion there and, while the zen approach still eases the stress, it's impossible not to care.

> # NONE OF THOSE ESCALATING, FRUSTRATED THOUGHTS WILL SPEED THE TRAFFIC UP. SO WHY THINK THEM?

Beware food rules

Some people are unfortunate enough to have very complex and unhealthy issues in their relationship with food. Many of us have some underlying beliefs or attitudes that colour the relationship, and which it helps to recognise. So here are a few of the more common and unhelpful patterns we can get into as a result of the way we relate to food.

I've already touched on the first, which is the inability to leave food on your plate[30]. You don't have to have grown up in the 1950s and 60s, or in the West, to have been taught from an early age that you must finish everything on your plate. At school we were never allowed to leave the table until every last morsel was eaten. My headmistress when I was about five would say, 'Don't leave anything on your plate. Think of all the starving children'. I could never understand at that age how they would be helped by me clearing my plate. Surely it would be better to leave something and they could have it?[31]

It's interesting how the human mind works. There were lots of other rules when I was young which would serve most of us very well now, and which somehow failed to embed themselves into my psyche: never eat between meals, never eat in the street (or in the car), it's good to feel hungry before a meal. From observation I'm not the only person whose mind glossed over these less welcome rules.

Here's another childhood admonishment you may have heard: 'You can't have pudding unless you finish your main course.' This translates broadly in your subconscious as 'Sweet things are wonderful and you can't have them unless you work through the tedious savoury stuff first'. It's not actually healthy to grow up believing sweet foods are inherently much nicer than savoury foods, but that's what happens if you are raised by this rule.

---

[30] *The Rules of Living Well* Rule 48: Understand your issues
[31] I do now understand that her point was about gratitude, not logistics

Alongside this rule is the broader implication that all meals should be rounded off with something sweet. That can be a hard habit to break after you grow up – always wanting something sugary to follow. Incidentally, the only way I could find to avoid passing this on to my own children was not to give them any kind of pudding at all (except fruit) unless we had visitors.

Here's another common unhealthy rule, often perpetrated by primary schools as well as parents: sweet or unhealthy foods as a reward or compensation. For winning a race, or because you fell over and hurt your knee, or because you completed your homework or cleaned your room or walked the dog. Eighteen years of that, and you turn into an adult who tells themselves, 'I need chocolate, I've had a bad day,' or 'I deserve a treat, I worked hard at that presentation.' There's nothing wrong with eating the occasional unhealthy treat – the problem comes when you associate it with a particular behaviour. Much better for treats to be completely random, or perhaps associated with rare occurrences (holidays or Christmas or cinema trips) so they can't happen too often.

Oh, but not so rare they become deeply sought after. Tricky stuff this, eh?

> # THERE'S NOTHING WRONG WITH EATING THE OCCASIONAL UNHEALTHY TREAT – THE PROBLEM COMES WHEN YOU ASSOCIATE IT WITH A PARTICULAR BEHAVIOUR

Enjoy your mistakes

Mistakes are good. We like mistakes. We *love* mistakes. Mistakes are how we learn, how we improve next time. They make our neural pathways spark into finding a better solution. It's said that you can't ride properly until you've fallen off a horse at least three times. That's not because you're supposed to fall off the horse. No, falling off the horse is certainly a mistake. And you have to do it in order to learn. So when it comes to learning new skills, embrace those mistakes.

I quite like cooking. I have even – very rarely – been known to cook puff pastry (I know, what's the point, you can buy it ready-rolled at the supermarket, don't know what I was thinking). Puff pastry is supposed to be tricky to cook, but it always worked for me. It rose light, fluffy and buttery every time. And that worried me, because I knew it was tricky, and I didn't really understand how I was getting it right. Eventually, after years of cooking it (albeit only about once a year) I took it out of the oven and it was heavy and soggy. At last! I *knew* it was tricky! I investigated where I'd gone wrong – turned out I'd let it get too warm before going in the oven, if you're interested – and finally I felt I understood how to cook it. No longer did I have to feel I was succeeding by fluke. I actually knew what I was doing. Funnily enough, that was the point when I started buying the ready-rolled stuff from the supermarket. Maybe I felt the challenge had evaporated. There was no satisfaction left in getting it right when I knew before I started that it would go fine.

Most schools don't encourage mistakes. Most bosses don't really like you to make them. They all know that we're supposed to learn from our mistakes, but really they'd rather we didn't make our mistakes on their time. But hang on . . . you're in charge now. This is your learning, for you, and no one else cares about your mistakes. So you can make as many as you like. So what? Every mistake will show you where you need to focus if you want to improve, and that's really useful. And you can enjoy the fact that it's no one's business but yours.

Whether you're serious about gaining a qualification, or just trying your hand at a new skill to see how it goes, your mistakes will tell you whether you're pushing yourself too hard, not concentrating because it's too easy, finding one particular area tricky, better in the mornings, better around other people, can't focus when there's background noise, need to read up on a bit of info, should be more patient (that's one of my regulars) . . . the more value you can get from your mistakes, the more you'll enjoy making them.

So relish your mistakes, embrace them, laugh at them. I can remember trying to hang wallpaper for the first time, with my sister – now that was a learning curve and no mistake. About the first half dozen attempts were genuinely laughable. In fact I can remember a lot of giggling about how badly we were doing. But I learnt loads (mostly that actually I really like my walls painted).

RELISH YOUR MISTAKES, EMBRACE THEM, LAUGH AT THEM

Create boundaries

If you have a colleague, or indeed a mother or a friend, who always does anything you ask of them happily, you're going to keep asking, aren't you? I mean, why wouldn't you? You need the help, and it doesn't seem to bother them, so of course you're going to see if they could just cover for you for a few minutes, or cast their eye over this report, or have a word with the boss on your behalf. Or in the case of family and friends you might ask them to pick up some shopping for you while they're out, or to mind the kids for a few minutes.

That works both ways round. If you're similarly happy to help other people, they're much more likely to ask you. And up to a point, that's fine. The thing is, they don't know where that point is – the point beyond which it isn't fine. Only you know that. So you need to let them know too, or they'll be asking for things that aren't really OK.

Also, that point moves around, so one day it might be easy to cover for your colleague but tomorrow it might not. How are they meant to understand that? I'll tell you: they aren't meant to, and they won't. If you agree to stay late at work today, your boss *will* assume it's OK to ask you again next week. Yes, even if you did lamely say 'just this once'. They won't hear that bit – that's human nature. So you need clear ground rules, and you need to stick to them. Yes, even on the days when it really is fine to help out, because you don't want to set a precedent.

Of course it's great to be as helpful as you can to other people within your parameters, and you choose what those parameters are. Maybe you need a good 30 minutes for lunch but not the whole hour. Maybe you're genuinely happy to stay late occasionally, so long as it's no later than 6 pm. Or only in the few days running up to a big presentation or exhibition or event. Establish your parameters in cold blood, not in the heat of the moment.

Know in advance what you will and won't say no to. For example, you might be firm about working only 9 to 5, or not checking emails in the evening or at weekends. It's definitely good for your mental health to insist that your annual leave is a total break from work with no checking of emails at all. Another excellent rule is that you won't ever take work home with you – that one can turn into a very slippery slope.

I realise that some of these suggestions are going to sound completely ridiculous if you work in, say, a high-pressure job in the City, where it's taken as read that you'll work late every evening and be on call 24/7. I'll be frank, I don't approve of asking that much of employees in any job, but I know it happens. Nevertheless there will still be colleagues who are more put-upon than others, and you need to make sure you're not one of them. If you love the job, that's fine. If it doesn't make you happy, you might want to talk to your boss about parameters that could work for you both, if they don't you want you to either leave or burn out somewhere down the line.

> # IF YOU AGREE TO STAY LATE AT WORK TODAY, YOUR BOSS *WILL* ASSUME IT'S OK TO ASK YOU AGAIN NEXT WEEK

RULE 8

Stay in synch

Are you one of those people who wakes up and, bang, you're into your day? You check your emails before you get out of bed, think about your first meeting while you're still in the shower, wolf down a piece of toast on your way out of the door? Lots of us do it. We're barely aware of ourselves going through the motions of washing, dressing, breakfasting, because our mind is an hour ahead of our body.

It's so easy to do, especially when life is busy or work is demanding. But you're really not living in the present, are you? You might think you work an eight-hour day, but you can stick another hour or two on to the beginning of that. And mostly a fairly unproductive couple of hours, too. How much can you honestly achieve while you're showering, or cleaning your teeth? Is that email really so urgent that your reply couldn't wait until 9 am?

It's when work is stressful or challenging that it's most important you don't do this. You're giving yourself no breathing space, no time to relax and chill at the start of the day, and you're not even achieving much either. So keep your mind where your body is. Think home thoughts. Focus on enjoying your shower or your breakfast or your partner or kids.

You don't have to get up any earlier to do this – goodness knows, I'm not one to advise anyone to get up earlier than they have to. Nope, not a morning person, me. So unless you want to, you don't need to change your routine. It's just about where your mind is while you're doing it. Worrying about the bits of the day that haven't happened yet is not only fruitless but also bad for your mental health.

In an ideal world, you won't start thinking about work until you get there. After all, they don't pay you until you get there, so why should you? Read a book on your commuter train, listen to a podcast in the car, enjoy the weather as you walk or cycle. I appreciate that there will be the occasional one-off day when you want to prepare mentally for a big interview or presentation that day, but that should be a rare occasion, and one where you use the time really productively – to plan or rehearse, not to worry and fret.

Are you still worrying about that email you can't reply to until 9 am? Well, don't. For a start you don't know it exists because you're not looking at your emails before you arrive at work, remember. And here's part two of keeping your body and mind synchronised: when you get to work, give yourself time to get up to speed. If you have any control over your day, schedule 30 minutes or an hour clear to prepare for the day and get anything urgent out of the way. So *now* you can check your emails.

Your colleagues will learn that you're not available before 9.30am unless it's urgent. If your workplace kicks off on the dot and there's not much you can do about it, try getting in half an hour early so you can get your head round the day in peace before it starts. Oh alright, you might have to get up a bit earlier – for which you have my undiluted sympathy – but you know what? You'll feel so much better for it. I've had to do it myself in some jobs and (whisper it) it's still worth it.

> # IN AN IDEAL WORLD, YOU WON'T START THINKING ABOUT WORK UNTIL YOU GET THERE

RULE 9

Redraw your relationship

If you live with a partner, retirement is going to have a big impact on your relationship. I've seen it cause disruption and even divorce, and I've seen it bring couples closer together. The way to ensure the latter is to think through the possible consequences together, and to draw up a new set of ground rules – oh, and keep it flexible because some things may not work out the way you expect. As with all good relationships, communication is going to be essential.

What will these new ground rules be? Well, that's up to you, but I can give you an idea of the areas that I've observed often need to change. Perhaps the key one is the division of labour in the house, and this is trickier if one of you hasn't been going out to work for a while.

The biggest problem I see is when the overall workload has previously been split fairly equally: one of you has gone out and earned all the money, while the other one has done everything in the house – laundry and shopping and cleaning and cooking. Between the two of you, that's a reasonable way to divide up the effort needed to keep the family unit running smoothly. When the 50 per cent money-earning share of this workload stops, the logical thing is to redistribute the other 50 per cent of the workload equally across both members of the team. And problems can arise when that doesn't happen, because if the stay-at-home member of the team is expected to carry on as before, suddenly their contribution feels really unfair. Because it is. So if you're the one retiring, you have to recognise that there will be new responsibilities at home.

However – and this is a big 'but' – the stay-at-home partner is likely to cause resentment if they think they've just acquired a junior assistant to do their bidding. No one wants to go from running a department to being told they haven't hoovered 'properly'.

It's not easy handing over areas of responsibility, even if you embrace the idea of sharing your workload, but it is essential that you do hand over responsibility fully, and don't just delegate tasks. Agree between you what division of labour you think will work before you start, and then be flexible and keep reviewing. You'll need to be honest if you know you can't stand having someone else in 'your' kitchen, or if you think you're being given all the boring jobs.

You'll also need to navigate other areas such as how much time you spend together – and what you do with it – and how much privacy you each need now you're both at home most of the time. You might need to create your own spaces, or perhaps only one of you might. You don't have to have the same rules for each of you, you know, unless you want them.

It's probably easiest to make retirement work when you both retire almost simultaneously. But it's perfectly possible to make the change to a happy and successful retirement however it comes about, so long as you both make an effort to stay on the same page, and to compare notes regularly and voice any reservations as they arise. The most important thing, whether you're the one retiring or not, is to have a clear eye on the other one's point of view.

> NO ONE WANTS TO GO FROM
> RUNNING A DEPARTMENT TO
> BEING TOLD THEY HAVEN'T
> HOOVERED 'PROPERLY'

Forgive and don't forget

Who are you still angry with, or maybe just quietly seething about below the surface? Who is it that you don't want to let off the hook, don't want to accept their explanations, don't think deserves to be forgiven? They need to be punished for what they've done to you, or to the people you love, and you need to go on being angry or bitter or resentful towards them. Maybe your mother or father were terrible parents, perhaps your business partner cheated you, maybe your child never visits you, or your partner had an affair.

Some people hold many grudges and some have just one or two major ones. It's tempting to feel that so long as you bear a grudge, or continue to apportion blame, or keep reliving the hurt, you can keep punishing the person who has wronged you. But wait a minute, who exactly are you punishing? I'd say the person suffering most is you. Feelings of anger, bitterness, resentment . . . they're no fun. They buzz around inside your head like a swarm of stinging bees. You've already been hurt enough – why do you deserve to live with this feeling too?

It's easy to resist forgiving someone because we feel that by doing so we are saying the offence didn't matter, or is forgotten. Of course it matters, and by forgiving someone you're not saying you'll forget – the expression 'forgive and forget' has a lot to answer for. The two don't in any way have to go together.

Forgiveness is ultimately about acceptance[32] and you're doing it for you, not for them. Once you acknowledge that you can't change the past, and that you have to find a way to live with it and adapt to it, you will feel freer and happier, which is no more than you deserve.

You don't even have to tell the other person you've forgiven them – if you ever even let them know you were angry with them.

---

[32] *The Rules of Living Well* Rule 96: It is what it is

You might never have told your parents that you blame them for your unhappy childhood. On the other hand, you might have had a massive falling out with a friend over the way they treated you. But this isn't about them, so once you've forgiven them, it's up to you what you do with the information. Either way, you're not going to forget your childhood, nor trust your friend in quite the same way again. But you have accepted the past.

Personally, I learnt to forgive my mother once I saw my childhood years from her perspective. I realised she can't have been happy herself, wasn't cut out for parenthood (least of all on her own with half a dozen children), and didn't think to consider the impact her methods would have on all of us – which in fairness wasn't a thing parents thought about nearly so much in the 1950s and 60s. A bit of understanding can go a long way to accepting someone else's behaviour, without having to justify it.

So have a bit of kindness and consideration . . . for yourself. Find a way to come to terms with what's happened and to leave it in the past. Not forgotten, but accepted. Close the file, and archive it safely, where you can look at it when you need to without having to rummage and ruckle and rearrange it. Aaaahhh – doesn't that feel better?

> ## YOU WILL FEEL FREER AND HAPPIER, WHICH IS NO MORE THAN YOU DESERVE

KNOW WHEN TO BREAK THE RULES

This is actually the final Rule from The Rules of Work – *the very first Rules book – and received several nominations. However it's applicable to every book in the series and I thought it would be helpful to include it here as an end note...*

Life doesn't run to a neat and infallible formula. Sometimes the unexpected happens. And the true Rules Player has the confidence, the understanding and the presence of mind to recognise those moments and to break the Rules.

Many excellent and committed Rules Players I meet start out following every Rule slavishly. When you're first setting out, this is a sensible approach. After all, the alternative is complacency and an assurance that 'I can do this stuff', which certainly isn't true. None of us finds every situation effortless. It may be clear what we should do, but that doesn't always mean it's easy. And sometimes we're not even sure which way to go.

So, by all means start out taking each Rule seriously. That's the general idea. However, as you become more comfortable and self-assured as a Rules Player, and begin to develop sound instincts for Rules behaviour, you can begin to loosen up. Many of the Rules will become automatic and you'll no longer have to think about them. And once you reach this stage, you'll find that occasionally, just occasionally, one of the Rules really isn't quite appropriate.

It's no good persuading yourself a Rule doesn't fit because you'd much rather not have to follow it. You need to be clear and objective. But when your instincts genuinely tell you to break a Rule, then go for it.

Personally, I find that there's rarely a need to break a Rule. It's not a daily occurrence, or even a weekly one (at least not on purpose – of course, I'm not perfect and I still look back on my day and feel I should have handled some bits of it better). But I do break them occasionally. For example, a Rules Player never deliberately belittles other people in public, but about twice in my life I've encountered people who really needed to be belittled in public to stop them from doing it to others, and I've been happy to oblige.

Look, in the end it's about gut feeling. Follow the Rules until they're so ingrained they become instinct, and then trust your instincts. If you refer back to the Rules from time to time (not only these Rules but others you encounter in life too) to make sure you're not forgetting or misinterpreting them, and you work on the ones you find tricky, you can be confident that in time your instincts will serve you better than any book.

> ## FOLLOW THE RULES UNTIL THEY'RE SO INGRAINED THEY BECOME INSTINCT, AND THEN TRUST YOUR INSTINCTS

Create your own Rules

Remember, I'm not the only one who can observe other people and see what works for them that could work for me too. So keep a look out for new Rules, and when you identify one I haven't included here, note it down. Keep a list of additional Rules you want to emulate and write them down. You can share them too so we all benefit.

If you're wondering what makes a good Rule, it's a guiding principle that works in (almost) all cases for people of all kinds. It's not just a handy trick or a useful tip (for example, use coloured stickers to organise yourself, or keep your car de-icer in the house and not the car – you always need it when you're at home anyway, and that way the bottle isn't freezing cold – or never eat anything bigger than your head). Useful as these pointers are, they're not Rules in the sense I use the word. A good Rule is about changing your attitude or shifting your mindset so you approach problems or situations from a different perspective.

It seems a shame to keep these new Rules to yourself, so please feel free to share them with other people. If you'd like to share them on my Facebook page I'd love to hear from you at www.facebook.com/richardtemplar. Either post a single Rule, or maybe put together your top five and post them so other readers can get the benefit.

When you decide to share a Rule, it's a good idea to explain it, and then to give an example or two so other people can see how it works in practice, to help them understand how to apply it to their own lives.

A Rule is a Rule, it doesn't matter whether it's me or you or anyone else who has noted it down (in fact, it doesn't matter if no one has identified it yet, it's still a Rule). If it works, not only for you but for other people too, it's worth sharing. So please post your new Rules and, who knows, I may even assemble the best of them together sometime in the future.

Printed in Great Britain
by Amazon